UNTOUCHED

MIRACULOUS RECOVERY

JOAN E. ANDERSON

Library of Congress Control Number:

ISBN eBook: 978-1-960995-23-0

ISBN Paperback: 978-1-960995-22-3

Printed in the United States of America.

Author Disclaimer: I have tried to recreate events, locales and conversations from my memories of them.

CONTENTS

INTRODUCTION

My life story is very important to me as I experienced something many other babies born in the late 1930s did as well. Due to the child-raising practices in the year of my birth, I was untouched as a newborn baby but survived. My life had many ups and downs, but God's interventions brought supernatural miracles throughout my entire life.

With the events of the world today, there is much unrest, as there was throughout my life. I want to share how God delivered me from the emotional trauma that the lack of physical love and attention caused during the first year of my life. Although I was untouched during that first year, I was fully loved thereafter. But the effects of the first year were devastating. I attribute no fault to my parents, since they thought they were doing the right things for me. I learned to love and forgive.

In this book, I share with you the events of my lifetime and how the Lord enabled me to become completely free to forgive, forget, love and move on. This is an exciting time to share with you - my reader. There were so many good times, as well as difficult times, but all worked out to perfection.

My siblings and I were born into a segregated city – Wilmington, Delaware – but lived in a non-segregated neighborhood. We were a fairly wealthy family as my father was a doctor, so we gave to others who were less fortunate. My life spanned the great depression, the war years, racial unrest, as well as a time of great inventions like the electronic computer.

I had varied careers ranging from roles in soap operas to success in the business world, but my involvement in integrating schools and being one of the plaintiffs in the now famous Brown vs. Board of Education case was ny most extraordinary and exciting venture, even to this day.

I would like those who read this book to find encouragement in knowing that whatever your circumstances, there is always healing in the Lord.

I hope my stories of the pet chicken, the dog tales and the cookie monster will bring a smile to your face. I pray that you will enjoy reading about my life and experiences.

Blessings and love,

Joan

Chapter 1 My First Two Years

"Oh, what a beautiful baby!" my family members exclaimed. My Aunt Annie asked, "May I hold her?" Others looked eagerly at me, wanting to touch me.

"Oh, no!", my mother cried out, as she arrived home from the hospital, still holding me, her second child, in her arms. "Absolutely not! Don't you know you shouldn't touch babies in their first year, except for tasks like feeding, diaper changing, and putting to bed?"

I imagine it would have been a beautiful day, full of sunshine, flowers blooming - a Blessed day. It had to have been a day of lovely events, because a very special person would soon be born. The world was preparing the way for a beautiful baby. That baby was me - Joan Elizabeth Anderson. The date was August 10, 1938.

Shocking? Well, in the 1920s and 1930s, doctors advised parents against hugging, kissing, or cuddling children because such fawning might create weak and needy children. Instead, they felt the babies would grow to be strong and independent adults without the cuddling. The doctors believed the children could handle the new way of being raised.

Child-rearing experts in the early 1900s promoted detachment. "Never hug and kiss them, never let them sit in your lap." John B. Watson wrote in his book "Behaviorism." He went on to say, "If you must, kiss them once on the forehead when they say goodnight. Shake hands with them in the morning."

This was the theory under which I was born and cared for during my first year of life.

This concept continued until after World War II when Dr. Benjamin Spock wrote a book titled, "Baby and Child Care", which became an international bestseller with 50 million copies sold in his lifetime. The book discouraged the "hands-off" theories of the day. Instead, Spock appealed to parents to give each of their children plenty of physical affection.

The Bible verse says, "Children are a heritage from the Lord." Psalm 127:3 NKJV. I remember when my siblings were born. I smiled when my mother laid the babies in my arms to hold. It was a joy.

I was shocked to find out that my birth took place in a time of sad events - the great depression, famines, earthquakes, poverty, and racial unrest. These were not happy times. Why me? This should have been a time of joy rather than deep sorrow and depression.

I wish I could have been a happy baby, laughing and clapping my hands with joy. A baby who knew that when she cried, help was on the way. But, for me, things were different. This theory changed my development. I was unaware of how this would affect my life. After all, I had just been born.

I was too young to understand that a book was raising me, and other babies were suffering the same neglect. This experiment lasted the first full year of my life. Then some doctors changed their minds about raising babies. Suddenly, I began to get attention. People held and cuddled me, which made me very happy - until they put me down. Then, I would cry and get angry until someone picked me up again. This went on for another year until, at age 2, I finally decided to walk. I needed a lot of love. I didn't know at the time that Jesus was there, for He said, "And lo, I am with you always." Matthew 28:20. KJV. But I also needed others to be there.

After my oldest sister Merle and I were born, there was yet another newborn, my sister Carol. She took a lot of my mother's time. So, the loving touch I wanted and needed slipped away again. Also, my father being a doctor meant he wasn't home a lot. In those times, doctors were not only general practitioners, but they performed other medical services. He also was a surgeon and an obstetrician. He would put our fun trips, vacations and activities on hold while caring for his patients. None of us were happy about that because our fun had to wait for babies to make their entrance into the world.

After Carol, there were three more children, Linda, Victor and Alicia. Our household was getting crowded, and I was kind of lost in the mix. It wasn't anyone's fault; it was the times we were living in. All six children were born close in age and demanded my mother's time.

Me at age one with my mother.

Due to the circumstances, I became angry and fearful. I cried almost continually, even with outbursts of screaming and throwing things.. My parents did their best to help me. But it was overwhelming. It was always upsetting to hear that my mother was pregnant again as I knew there would be less time for me. So, I would stand in front of her and cry as loud as I could. It didn't really work, because she learned to tune me out and continued reading her book. Recently, I heard the Lord say to me, "I was there all the time. I'm God Almighty, and I love all of my little children." But at the time, I could not be soothed. As time went by, my screams subsided., but the wound remained. Only God could heal it. He knew that later as I grew older, I would understand.

This age in which I was born and raised was different. There were no longer three classes of people-wealthy, middle class, and the poor. My generation was called the Have's and the Have not's. There was really no middle class. You were either wealthy or poor. My Father was considered wealthy. In addition to his medical practice, he also co-owned an apartment building. Growing up, we never had to go without the basic necessities. However, my parents gave to the needy, and taught us to do so.

This was also the age of women wearing long dresses and matching shoes and bags. My mother looked beautiful and my father looked handsome in his suits with matching ties. I remember them as a good-looking couple as they went out on their usual Friday outings, leaving us to endure a babysitter.

While writing my autobiography, I have enjoyed learning about the amazing events that happened during the year of my birth. These were exciting times - The New York Yankees became World Series champions; the New York Giants won the NFL East in the 1938 season and Chicago Blackhawks won the Stanley Cup. There were cowboy movies featuring Gene Autry and The Adventures of Robin Hood. In addition, ballpoint pens and Teflon were introduced. The cost of living in the 1930s was stunning. A new house cost $3,900.00. The average rent was $27.00 per month. And the average income was $1,731.00 per year. What a change to today's prices.

Due to my loneliness, I demanded even more attention. My parents did their best to help me. But it was overwhelming. Recently, I heard the Lord say to me, "I was there all the time. I'm God Almighty. and I love all of my little children. You are of the kingdom of heaven." He knew that, later, as I got older, I would change and the screams would stop.

One exciting thing about writing my autobiography was reviewing all the enjoyable events that took place during the year I was born. The New York Yankees became World Series champions, the New York Giants won the Super Bowl and Chicago won the Stanley Cup. There were cowboy movies featuring Gene Autry, and The Adventures of Robin Hood. In addition, ballpoint pens and Teflon were introduced.

***

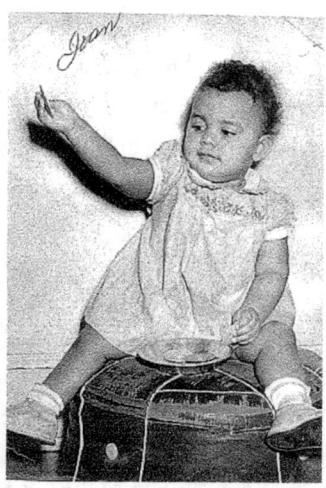

Me at two years old enjoying and sharing some cookies.

Throughout my first two years, I became easily agitated and more fearful; throwing fits and lashing out at people. I know I was a crybaby and got attention that way. I really needed help, and it seemed there was none. But today, I know Jesus was there. Without His help, I wouldn't be here today. It has been a long road, but I can see how He has guided me to the help that I needed, which is In Him. This book will show the progression of my journey to total healing.

As I researched more about children like me in the 30s, I was shocked at what I read, as below from Psychology Today: "Hugs, Your Child Crave Them":

"Many long for the presence of caring touch in their daily life and its absence can cause loneliness, insecurity, and stress. Caring touch is of great importance to your mental and physical well-being, "The Overlooked Human Need." If your children are not touched, they can get into a deficit state that can lead to negative mental health and show up as psychosomatic symptoms. These symptoms could include a headache, abdominal pain, anxiety, and sadness, to name a few." Dec 15, 2019. "Many children who have not had ample physical and emotional attention are at higher risk of behavioral, emotional and social problems as they grow up." May 6, 2010.

I now know why I had so many problems, and I can see the God's miracles as l grew up. I am thankful.

Chapter 2 The War Years

The times became more difficult. World War II loomed and men faced the draft while others enlisted. Mothers cared for their families, and many found work to feed their families. Some children were even left to care for themselves. My mother, who now had six children, was already taking care of us by herself as my father was so busy.

Thankfully, my father wasn't drafted. He was on the staff of the local hospital and had a private practice with some members of the famous Dupont family as his patients. There wasn't much medical segregation since there was only one hospital. Sometimes, my father would bring home food and other forms of payment for medical services. There were times when the extreme poverty caused by the war left people with no cash, only bartering.

Black people suffered immensely. Many children were not able to attend school and there were few jobs causing racial unrest. According to Encyclopedia Britannica, in early public assistance programs, they often received substantially less aid than Whites, and they were the first to be laid off from their jobs.

This intensified economic plight sparked major political developments among the Black race. Beginning in 1929, the St. Louis Urban League launched a national "Jobs for Negroes" movement by boycotting chain stores that had mostly Black customers but hired only White employees. Efforts to unify Negro organizations and youth groups later led to the founding of the National Negro Congress in 1936 and the Southern Negro Youth Congress in 1937.

Food lines were commonplace.

Food lines helped those who could not find jobs Churches and private companies and families like mine also helped. The few food lines in the cities helped, too.

I knew we were fortunate to have a nice big house to live in. The backyard was large with pear and apple trees. There was also a big open area to play ball. We always had fresh vegetables from our garden. We ate tomatoes, carrots, lettuce, and beets. We especially enjoyed our pear and apple trees except when it came time to harvest the fruit. This job fell to us children, and it was hard work. We loved the fruit, but dreaded harvest season.

We were young and growing up in this way, made it difficult to understand the racial/political environment. I was enjoying a nice place to live and playing with neighborhood children. But I could still see the economic plight of my fellow members of the Black race.

With all of us kids close in age, Dad gave Mom help with a maid service, which made us happy because we did not have to clean the house. But we did take turns cooking meals. As we grew older, Mom let the maids go and sent us to our knees to clean the house. We weren't happy about it. In fact, we were angry and grumbled as we mopped floors and scrubbed toilets. We declared that when we had our own children, we were not going to make them do the work. Looking back on this, I could see why Mom just smiled at us. She knew these were lessons we needed to learn.

Our parents were always looking for ways to help people. At some point they decided to use the services of the local institution for wayward children. In exchange for help around the house, the young teenagers got free meals and an allowance. We loved them and were excited they were there, especially since they did some of the work!

According to The Encyclopedia Britannica, the industrial boom that began with the outbreak of the War in Europe in 1939 which ended the Great Depression. Factories converted to build the war machine. It was also a time of inventions of many things we enjoy today—the jet engine, the computer, the microwave oven, kitty litter, big bands, color TV, the Jeep, and mobile phones.

But Black Americans didn't share equally in this bounty. There was still wide-spread job discrimination and poverty. Members of the Brotherhood of Sleeping Car Porters threatened a mass protest march on Washington. In advance of the march, scheduled for June 25, 1941, President Roosevelt banned "discrimination in the employment of workers in defense industries or government" and established a Fair Employment Practices Committee (FEPC) to investigate violations. Although discrimination remained widespread during the war, members of the Black race began to secure more jobs at better wages and in a greater range of occupations than ever before.

Finally, the war was almost over though we still had air raid drills which are unforgettable. When we heard the siren, we would run to the windows, draw the dark shades down, and head to the basement until we heard the all-clear siren. We also did this in schools. The drills happened often throughout those years

Then suddenly came the announcement that the war was over! I remember the day it happened because there were massive celebrations. Everyone danced in the streets, smiling, laughing, and shouting with joy. People jumped up and down and hugged each other. It's a day no one could forget.

However, I still had bouts of anger, temper tantrums and rebelled against rules and instructions. My parents did all they could for me, but I was very fearful and often hid especially at night. I was still hurting inside.

Recently, I heard Jesus say, "I was there at those times. When you were hiding at night, I would wake your older sister and tell her to wake your parents and let them know you were missing again. Each time, I would show them where you were—under the bed, in the closet, or under the bureau. There was one time when you were under the bed and your hair caught in the springs. You woke up screaming, and I showed them how to cut you loose. I really was there all the time."

Psalm 46:1b NKJV tells us "God is our refuge and strength, A very present help in trouble." I know it to be true.

Jesus told me, "Often, when you would wander, sleepwalking, and sit in the chair next to your mother's side, I would wake her so she would send you back to bed. You needed sleep." As Psalm 127:2 NKJV says, "For so

He gives His beloved sleep." It was only when my mother woke up that I woke up. I remember those times of waking up sitting next to her.

My parents installed a gate at the top of the stairs so I would not fall in my sleepwalking state. They discussed sending me to a mental institution, but my mother rejected that idea. The mental institution was not a good option, because in those days if you went In, you never came out. Looking back, I can hear Jesus say, "I, the Lord, stopped them, I had another way; knowing you would one day receive Jesus as your savior and the real healing would begin. For now, you will see me doing good things for you as you grow - even though you may not know it is me."

The outbursts of anger started to diminish a little over time. I began to withdraw instead and tried to create a safe and secure world inside myself. I still had difficulty socializing with family and friends. It was during these dark days that Jesus was guiding me and later became my savior.

CHAPTER 3 MY ELEMENTARY YEARS

In those years, I grew physically and enjoyed excelling in sports, but mentally, I still had challenges. My sister Merle and I took piano lessons. Merle excelled in classical piano and Carol, my other sister, studied violin and was exceptional at classical music. I played classical piano as well, but due to a crooked finger on my right hand, I could only touch the keyboard with nine fingers. Nobody noticed until I was older. I remember the day my music teacher realized it and was shocked. She could hardly believe it and had never seen anything like it before! My father was also amazed. I had played many years with it. My music career didn't advance too far. I really needed that little finger.

Problems and issues seemed to follow me, and I was still fearful and angry at times. Once I was so angry at one of my siblings that I threw a softball at her, hitting her hard. I was trying to get back at her for something that I can't even remember now. The outcome of it was that no one in my family would have anything to do with me. I was alone again. There were many of these lonely times with everyone shunning me.

As I'm writing this, I hear Jesus speaking through the Holy Spirit. I hear Him say, "I was always with you during your lonely times when you were young." Matthew 28:20 says, "I am with you always." It's special to know that during those lonely years, I really was never alone. Jesus was always guiding me.

There were times when I was happy. Christmas was always one of those times. It was a favorite time since our families took turns hosting the dinner. For some of my relatives, it was the only time we got together. We played games and enjoyed lots of great food. The main meal was always turkey, mashed potatoes, sweet potato and green beans, and, of course, delicious desserts like sweet potato pie. It was a festive and very happy time for us, and we all received gifts. One or two uncles would give us money which thrilled all of us. Our father also did the same.

Dad fixed a fancy Christmas breakfast with pastries, bacon, and eggs. There were other times he enjoyed cooking for us, too, and he was a surprisingly good cook. It was always a treat when he cooked for us – especially for Mom. Gift opening waited until after breakfast, and then came the time when we could descend upon our many Christmas presents. It was loads of fun, and we felt blessed with so much abundance.

Once I shocked my parents by asking if Santa brought us all these gifts, what did you and Dad give us? I can still see the shocked look on their faces, as they tried to figure how to answer. I think they were a little angry about it. My mother finally said, "Santa gave you the gifts and Dad and I gave you the clothes." That kept me believing in Santa until I was 9 years old. I was heartbroken to discover the truth because I thought I heard him on the roof! We always baked cookies for him. Now, we knew we were baking for Mom and Dad—no more cookies for them!

Our home in Wilmington, Delaware.

On Christmas evening, we piled into the car and Dad drove us around the neighborhood. We were awestruck by the beautiful lights and displays. Our home also had been well decorated, and people drove by to see it. We had spent much time decorating the windows with lights, and a wreath on our door. Inside we had a beautiful tall tree, full of bright bulbs and lights. Such fun times.

During these holiday times we also enjoyed visiting our many relatives. Seeing our Grandparents, aunts and uncles was fun since they gave us gifts. We had many cousins our age to play with. Our large family saw this as an opportunity to visit and get reacquainted.

We also enjoyed our two pets. Ming Toy was our dog's name. He was a medium-sized dog, part collie and part chow and very protective of us children. He stood between us and anyone who entered the house. It was a good thing that our father was a doctor, because he had to sew up many nipped ankles.

A chicken was our other pet. We loved him, and he loved us. We named him Andy. He didn't stay with us for very long. And no, the dog did not eat the chicken. In fact, they coexisted very well. The only bad part about having two pets was the cleanup. Some of us had to handle this awful chore, and we hated it.

There was one thing about the chicken - Andy was bold and fearless. We put the chicken's plate of food on one side of the pantry; and the dog's on the other side, and for a while this worked. Eventually Andy stopped eating his food and started eating the dog's food. A fight broke out, and we managed to save both pets. We separated them, putting the chicken under the house and making sure he was safe.

When we came home from school, we always checked on him. One day, we came home from school and couldn't find our beloved chicken. We looked everywhere. We quizzed our parents on it because our home was a fenced property. They told us someone left the gate open, and he ran away. We were gullible enough believe it.

We also didn't realize we were eating him that night. We found out later, and we were all mad at our parents. I held on to that anger for an awfully long time. At least our mother said she couldn't eat him. She apparently loved him, too. I wasn't a Christian yet and didn't know about forgiveness. I have since learned the importance of it.

At the time, depression and fear were a big part of my life. I disguised them as best I could. Either I didn't really know that I needed help or I was too afraid to ask for it. Occasionally, I would have outbursts of anger, but I kept trying to control it by retreating into my private world. If I got angry and couldn't express it, I would go into my father's pocket when he wasn't looking and take a nickel. It made me feel better. I did this whenever my anger erupted.

It was now time for me to enter first grade, and I felt traumatized by the changes in my life. I had never been away from home, and now I was dealing with different people—other students and a teacher. I was unable to communicate with her when I had to go to the bathroom, so I ended up going in my seat.

Of course, the reprimand didn't help. I was then sent to the kindergarten room to dry out. Now, I was alone with the little ones. My only consolation was that there was another student who had the same problem, and the teacher there was very nice to me.

There were other acts of kindness from those who favored me. I had an aunt who, whenever I saw her, she always hugged me and called me sweetie pie. Those were special times, and I looked forward to her visits. Every now and then, I experienced times of blessings when other people favored me and said nice things to me. I remember times when my father took me shopping for clothes and paid cash for them. Later after college, when I was living in New York, he would visit me. We would go to an upscale restaurant and then go sightseeing.

I'm constantly looking back now as I realize that someone **BIG (Jesus)** was always in my life. Someone who loved me. "To Him who loved us." Revelation 1:5 NKJV. Without the protection of Jesus, things would have been much worse.

My parents were strict in raising us and expected us to use our manners. Sometimes I was able to do so and sometimes not. When an elder person came into the room, we had to stand and remain standing until we were told to sit. I look back and realize these things were good. They kept me on the right path in being with others. I had my share of disciplines.

In the second grade, I was stronger and could finally ask to go the restroom, but it was still difficult to communicate with adults and some children. There came a time when I was chosen to be the princess on May Day and had to speak. I made it through without flubbing too much.

My parents also encouraged me and my siblings to take ballet lessons. I liked it okay, but I couldn't do the split. Others could, and it made me feel inferior. But I continued to try. Part of me was appreciative for the things my parents did for me.

By the 1940s, inventions like electronic computers, microwave ovens, iceboxes, and automatic washing machines were advancing and became available to the public over time, making life easier. The best was the washing machine. That made us all happy. We used to wash the clothes on a scrub board, by hand.

Some people then even had a color TV, and the Jeep was popular for transporting supplies. It later became an extremely popular car in America. Also, by 1944, most American households owned a refrigerator. Some of the foods produced back then are still popular today. We had Cheerios, Raisin Bran, Minute Rice, and Packaged Cake Mix.

Of course, the absolute best thing about the 40's was that the end of the war allowed us to move on to better times. I was growing and trying to do better and to make new friends through elementary school. I had some success, but I still withdrew with fearful bouts of anger, which made me want to seek revenge for wrongs I felt had been done to me, but I was having more success at controlling my emotions.

CHAPTER 4
MIDDLE YEARS

Now that elementary school was drawing to a close, I began to wonder and worry about how I would fit into junior high school at Howard High School. What would I do? The present environment made me feel at ease. I had adjusted and no longer wet my underwear. I could go to the restroom without being reprimanded, which had embarrassed me. I took comfort in the fact that my oldest sister, Merle, had just started attending Howard High School, and I would be next.

Being at Howard High school was challenging. I was a little older now, and I was expected to be more mature. But sitting in the first seat was awkward, and I got called upon more often. This was a prestigious school, and I didn't know if I could get good grades.

The Association for the Moral Improvement and Education of Colored People established Howard High School in 1867 and named it in honor of Civil War General Oliver Otis Howard. The original school was at 12th and Orange Street. Pierre S. DuPont was the major benefactor for the new building, which opened in 1928. With the annexation of the adjoining Howard Career Center in 1975, Howard's role as the major educational institution for Blacks expanded to include students from the total Delaware community.

Howard High school was the only Black High School in Delaware. The students who lived in Wilmington could get a high school education. Outside of the school district, education ended at the 6th grade level. However, a sixth-grade education was actually a very good education back in the mid-1940s, if you look up a test from back then.

My day to attend Howard High finally arrived, and I had to sit in the first seat, my last name being Anderson. One day, I had to verbally complete my information card. I was so frightened because I didn't know how to spell my middle name, Elizabeth. It was embarrassing, especially when word got back to my parents and siblings. They teased me unmercifully. It made me withdraw even more.

Howard High School had an excellent sports program, but I didn't participate. We loved attending football games since Howard High had an outstanding team. They were the best in the State. My parents provided music lessons and ballet lessons instead with a focus on classical music.

Our home became a favorite gathering spot for our large extended family because we had a big house and yard. My father's side had the most members. Grandmother was half English and half American Indian. We used to say she had no Indian blood—she was English all the way, taking after her all-English mother. One of my cousins said she was the spitting image of her mother. Grandfather was half White and half Black. I think he died when I was still a child. In those days, men often married younger women. When they married, my father was thirty-five and my mother was eighteen.

Upper row: my maternal great-grandmother, Sarah Margerum Dorrell was an English woman, who married a Mohawk man named John Walter Dorrell. Bottom row: Their daughter, Florence Dorrell Anderson married a Swedish man, Burnside Anderson and they lived a prosperous life in Wilmington, Delaware.

Great Grandmother
Annie Payne Anderson

My grandfather topped them all. He was thirty and his wife was only fifteen. Grandmother would sometimes visit us, especially after Grandfather died. We tried to keep our distance from her because she was very strict. She must have taken after her English mother, as she was quite formal. We were stiff as boards when we approached her. We had to stand and wait until we were told to sit. When addressing people, we had to use proper names. We spoke only when asked to speak. It didn't take us long to understand and maintain the routine. There were times, though, when we loved to come near to her. She had the most beautiful long, black Indian hair, which we loved to watch her brush. We learned to appreciate her ways.

It was quite a contrast between Grandmother Anderson and Grandmother Dyson, our mother's mom. We could jump and run around at the Dyson house. But we learned to fit into both worlds. We enjoyed both situations with many good times. I still remember when Grandmother Anderson died. It was upsetting and frightening to know we would never see her again. I know now that God welcomed her to heaven.

Grandmother and Grandfather Anderson had twelve children, and I had many cousins who lived close by. We saw them often. My parent's family valued education, and almost all of them had college degrees. Their parents also were also well-educated. This was in the 1940s when college degrees among Blacks were rare. Grandmother Anderson's mother graduated from finishing school and her husband developed a prosperous business. In my generation, we were all expected to go to college, and we did. The next generation was the followed suit.

Our Father was well-liked in the city of Wilmington. He donated to various charities and also accepted any form of payment from his patients for medical services. Once a year, he would provide a Thanksgiving dinner for everyone in the church. It was a big event that everyone attended. We kids were always excited about it, even though we had to work and serve the people. It was hard, but we didn't seem to mind.

Our parents took us to social events, like the Jack and Jill club. It was hard on me sometimes, because I was so shy, and didn't know how to socialize. It seemed no one wanted to dance with me. But they were still fun events. Some of my cousins also attended, and I enjoyed chatting with them.

The Jack and Jill Clubs, founded in 1938, were formative in many other children's lives. Hheadquartered in Washington, D.C., it is a leadership organization formed during the Great Depression by Black mothers wanting to bring together children in a social and cultural environment. The organization aims to improve the quality of life of children, particularly Black children. Now, Jack and Jill of America, Inc. boasts 262 chapters nationwide, representing over 50,000 family members - 10,000 mother members and 40,000 parents and children.

It all began in January 1938, when Marion Stubbs Thomas, a woman of mulatto ancestry, organized a group of twenty-one mothers in Philadelphia to establish a social and cultural union for their children. The group included many Black Catholics, one of the largest religious groups in Philadelphia.

They established the second chapter of Jack and Jill in New York City and a third in Washington, D.C., and many more between 1944 and June 1, 1946, when they established a national organization. It has created and funded many educational and charitable projects to benefit children and families across the United States.

Mothers of children between the ages of two and nineteen hold the membership and are required to plan and host monthly activities for the children. Children of all ages take part in cultural activities, fundraising, leadership training, legislative events, and social events. Mothers must be invited into the group and voted upon by the members.

Our family enjoyed the club, and there were many times I felt okay. I was happy when things went my way. Other times, I was still depressed and didn't know how to handle it. At times, I was punished or deprived of things I loved. My temper was still a problem, as I had difficulty controlling it. I took out my feelings mainly on my family. There were many times I would yell or throw things. Talking back to my parents was a no-no, but I did it anyway.

Pierre S. DuPont, President of E.I. DuPont de Nemours & Co. and General Motors in the 1920s, led the modernization of education for Black Americans in Delaware in a time of segregation and discrimination. DuPont drew attention to the problem of inadequate education by donating over $6 million of his own money to build new, state-of-the-art Schools.

Pierre S. DuPont was much loved by the Black community, because he built multiple identical schools in the community, and members of the Black community composed and sang a song, praising him .

I only spent two years at Howard High School. It was an eventful time. I still had emotional issues and was withdrawn. Jack and Jill took up a lot of time, as there was no Delaware chapter. We had to travel to other locations to attend the various events. We didn't seem to mind, since we could play with our cousins.

Famous Black Americans, such as historian W.E.B. DuBois and singer Marian Anderson, came to Howard High in the Black American community as guest speakers.

Marian Anderson, the legendary African American contralto, sang at the Lincoln Memorial on Easter Sunday in 1939 after she was refused a performance at Washington's Constitution Hall by the Daughters of the American Revolution because she was Black."

It was an extraordinary event having her and other guest speakers and singers. Everyone attended, standing room only.

School took up a lot of time during the week. On the weekends we always went to the movies at the only theatre for Black people. I remember enjoying the movies, especially the Westerns and Batman. Sometimes I got in for free by ushering. I liked this the most.

At church events, we socialized with other children. In those days, there were dances and parties. There was no dating, just chatting and sharing stories, laughing and playing games.

When TV entered our lives, we were not allowed to watch it during the week, only on the weekends. Our parents were concerned that we were becoming too mesmerized by it. Later in life, I had to make choices about programming, so I wouldn't spend my life on it. My past enabled me to do it. This was the prelude to the constant concern of parents today about too much screen time.

During those times, I existed in a mostly Black environment. Even though we lived in an interracial residential neighborhood, we associated mainly with family members and Black friends. That was the way of life.

Later, an extraordinary event took place. On September 12, 1960, at the Howard High School auditorium in Wilmington, Delaware, Dr Martin Luther King spoke at a public meeting sponsored by the local NAACP.

I was fortunate to be there and hear him speak. I had already graduated from Boston University and was temporarily living at my parent's home in Ardencroft. It was a passionate speech and the entire audience stood to give him a standing ovation.

He was involved in nonviolent protesting against southern segregation known as Jim Crow laws. He wanted to expose the problem to achieve Black equality and voting rights. Daily news reports swayed public opinion and convinced Americans that the civil rights movement was the most important issue of the time.

One of the most interesting things about Dr. King was his close relationship with Dr. Billy Graham. Dr King also helped break down color barriers in another way, by joining forces with a major movement to share the good news of Jesus Christ—Rev. Billy Graham's evangelistic crusades.

They both decided that they would not speak to segregated audiences. In 1953, despite segregation and racial tensions, Graham held an integrated crusade in Chattanooga, Tennessee. Hundreds of thousands of men, women, and children of all races sat together and worshiped the Lord.

"But when God looks at you, He doesn't look on the outward appearance; the Bible says He looks upon the heart," Graham preached.

In my era of the 1930s and 1940s, Howard High School was innovative, but segregated which was a continual source of frustration for Black parents in the Wilmington suburb of Claymont, Delaware. While their community had a well-maintained school in a picturesque setting with spacious facilities, Black children could not, by law, attend the Claymont School. Instead, they were transported daily on a 20-mile round trip to Howard High School located in an undesirable section of Wilmington.

At the end of the 1952 school year at Howard, my family moved to Ardencroft, Delaware, 2 miles south of Claymont. We were part of the effort to integrate, but I felt uprooted and didn't know what to expect. Even though I was from a segregated city, I had lived most of my life in a partially segregated residential area. Now I was going to live in an all-White environment. I was somewhat prepared, having experienced the integration in Wilmington.

CHAPTER 5 BROWN V. BOARD OF EDUCATION

I was born in one of 17 segregated states in the year 1938. In those days, women were expected to graduate from high school, get married, and raise children, as my mother did. My family expected that of me, and I accepted it. I was one of two women who graduated and went on to college. Most became homemakers.

I was the second of six children born to Leon and Beulah Anderson.

Linda, Victor, Alicia, Joan, Merle and Carol.

We lived in Wilmington, Delaware. Even though Wilmington had segregated areas, there were some residential areas that were integrated. My family lived in one on East 9th Street. I grew up playing with Blacks, Hispanics and White children. My father, being a medical doctor, worked in the local hospital in an integrated setting and attended to patients of all colors.

Leon and Beulah Anderson, my father and mother.

We lived in a large, two-story red brick house which was a fun house to play in with lots of nooks and crannies to explore. It also had an enclosed yard, big enough for playing sports and other games. We had one Black movie theatre, which was a Saturday favorite for me. With the help of my mother, they integrated the one white theatre before my family moved. We were among the first to see a movie there, and they treated us well.

I attended the only Black elementary school and later Howard High, for grades one through eight. I had adjusted to the segregation in Wilmington. As a child, I didn't think a thing about it, because it was just the way it was because of the segregation laws. Junior high school included seventh and eighth grades. However, I would be one of the first to enter an integrated school. Two lawsuits changed the law and allowed integration of two schools. The cases were Belton v. Gebhart and Bulah v. Gebhart in Delaware.

A favorite time for me was visiting relatives, especially our grandmother Pauline Dyson. She taught all grades — kindergarten through sixth — at State Line School in Claymont, Delaware. A nice, hilly walk, good for exercise, led to her one-room school for the Black students who lived on Hickman Row in Claymont. It amazed me to see all she could accomplish. She was a favorite grandmother to me, and I enjoyed those visits, which were many. I can still see her, on her knees, scrubbing the floors of the school. That was the kind of person she was, taking pride in everything that she undertook.

My Grandmother, Pauline Dyson, in front of her one-room, all-Black schoolhouse. State Line School.

Visits to her house were exciting times. I loved her house and enjoyed running all over it - upstairs, downstairs, and in every nook and cranny. She always had homemade baked goods that I loved. The aroma of those delicious rolls and other baked delicacies made our tummies growl. As I write this, I am still enjoying the sweet smells that filled her entire house.

Mealtime was a feast. She was an outstanding cook, no matter what she served us. Widowed, she enjoyed us kids as much as we did her. I hate to admit that going to her house also meant that we were relieved of housework or assisting with the meals. I think I helped out with washing the dishes. I also remember playing with the neighborhood children. Her house was on the right side of the road, where all the families were Black. The white families lived on the left. I don't remember seeing or playing with those children. Mainly, we connected to families on the right side, although grandmother did have contact with others.

Another thing I liked about Grandmother was that she would drive all the way into Wilmington to attend church with us. Sometimes we would come back to her home for a fabulous meal. It didn't get any better than this.

But even more special was that she was so nice to me. She never said a negative word to me. She really loved me, and I thank God for those who loved and cared about me as I was growing up.

Over time, I became more aware of her accomplishments. She was a great humanitarian, helping children and their families in all aspects, and providing additional food and clothing during the depression and war era. She extended her efforts into the larger community. She tutored many students and opened a thrift shop, which may still operate at the Claymont Community Center. She was youth choir director, Boy Scout leader, and Superintendent of Sunday Schools of the African Methodist Episcopal Church, Wilmington district, for twenty-eight years.

Claymont High: First white public school in Delaware to admit black students.

In addition, my grandmother played a primary role in making the 1952 integration of the Claymont schools successful — counseling students and working with the other school personnel. The superintendent of schools, Mr. Stahl, asked my grandmother to speak with the local parents to see if they wanted to send their children to Claymont High School. They all said yes, which was the foundation for the 1951 lawsuit — Belton v. Gebhart.

Meanwhile, my family was contemplating moving to Ardencroft, located 2 miles south of Claymont.

The community leaders of a town called Arden had contacted the local chapter of the NAACP, of which my father was a member, to see if he knew of any Black families who would want to live in Arden. My parents accepted the invitation.

The township of Arden included the towns of Arden, Ardencroft, and Ardentown. My parents had to build a house, which took a while, but we finally moved to Ardencroft in June 1952.

The neighborhood was completely White except for two other Black families who also moved there in the first effort to desegregate the area known as the three Ardens. The Arden Township also brought a family from China and set them up in the grocery business which was the only store. We received 100% acceptance there.

The area was heavily wooded, but we quickly learned how to go through a forested area with a creek, which had small but scary snakes in it. We navigated to the grocery store, but I was frightened and ran most of the way. I adapted to rural life. Most of the families were very friendly, and my siblings and I spent time in their homes and they in ours.

The drive to our new home on Veale Road was breathtaking - lined with beautiful tall trees, so tall that they formed an arch at the top. There was no fence, as at the Wilmington house, so our dog could bite some of the people who came to visit. There were no lawsuits in those days, but they got excellent medical care from my father.

After moving to Ardencroft, we faced the prospect of being bused to the all-Black Howard High School in Wilmington. However, our parents got involved in the school situation, which I watched with great anticipation.

By the end of the 1952 school year at Howard, I still didn't know which school I would attend in September. It made me a little nervous about my future. My parents were great, though, with their involvement and support.

The lawyers for the two lawsuits in 1951 were Louis L. Redding, who filed the cases, and Jack Greenberg, who assisted. The two lawsuits, Belton v. Gebhart and Bulah v. Gebhart, had Chancellor Collins J. Seitz presiding. He found for the plaintiffs based on the evidence and his visits to the schools.

Also, Thurgood Marshall became involved in the school desegregation cases. He was an American civil rights lawyer and jurist who served as an associate justice of the Supreme Court of the United States from 1967 until 1991. He was the Supreme Court's first African-American justice. (Wikipedia)

It was August now, and they had decided all Delaware cases for the plaintiffs, which required the issuance of a mandate for the schools to integrate immediately. Claymont was the only school that accepted all students eligible to attend grades seven through twelve, including those who were not part of the Belton case. It meant that I, along with my two sisters, Merle and Carol, would attend Claymont High.

This brought us great relief. The strange thing about all of this for me was to have first moved from an almost segregated environment (Wilmington) to an all-White environment (Ardencroft) and then on to an all-white school (Claymont). But all the decisions by my parents made us happy, and I knew I would continue to get an excellent education and make new friends.

It seemed all was going well in preparation for the opening school day. The Delaware Supreme Court rendered the final verdict on August 28, 1952. However, we needed a written mandate to attend, and the Attorney General's Office had not yet sent it. On September 3, 1952, I was getting a little anxious, because school was to begin the next day, and I wondered if I might still have to attend Howard High. But the Claymont School Superintendent, Mr. Harvey Stahl, defied the law and enrolled us on September 3, anyway.

I still remember being in his office on that day receiving his warm welcome. He also told the students and the faculty he would not allow any problems at his school. I was grateful because I feared there might be problems. That night, I felt anxious because we still didn't know which school we would attend, since our enrollment at Claymont was still not legal. Later that evening, we received a call that they had granted us a verbal mandate to attend Claymont, which legalized our attendance.

We all felt immediate peace at this resolution. On September 4, 1952, we entered Claymont and received a warm welcome from all, including from my new teacher. There were purposely no police or reporters to quell any potential disruption or violence. They kept it as quiet as possible. Whatever nerves I had quickly dissipated. Everyone was friendly. I remember my mother telling me that many of the staff and teachers hugged her and told her how happy they were that her children were attending Claymont High.

On September 5, 1952, Mr. Stahl received a call from Attorney General Young's office, telling him to send us home because we didn't have a written mandate to attend. Fortunately, he refused, and the teachers signed a petition that they wanted us to stay. Later that day, Mr. Young's office called to say we could stay, but that no other schools could integrate as they were preparing an appeal to the US Supreme Court to prevent further integration. I found out about it when I arrived home from school that day and was glad I could stay.

So many things were going on in my young life at that time. It was difficult to process everything mentally. My bouts of depression, fear, anger, and withdrawal from society continued. I didn't feel that anyone could really help me. Even though I could function okay, I remained the same. I built a house in my mind where I could escape.

I was trying to adjust to the school routines. The schedule was okay, and I made some friends. I immersed myself in the classes and homework, but I had problems comprehending all the lessons. Fortunately, my parents saw I needed help with the schoolwork. One of my uncles was a school teacher at Howard High school. He spent a lot of time with me because I was a slow learner.

Over 4 years, my math improved. But I had difficulty with taking exams. I would freeze up and not do well. My teachers recognized this and graded me more on my schoolwork than on the exams. In fact, some teachers would stop by to visit my family on a social call. I enjoyed the visits. I believe Jesus gave me favor with the staff, even though I didn't really know it. "In His favor is life." Psalm 30:5 KJB.

A couple of weeks into the school year, my two sisters and I had a situation we didn't know how to resolve. Being in an all-White school, we realized that our aunt (sounding like Ont) was no longer an aunt, but actually an Ant (spelled aunt). We didn't know what to do about it. Finally, we decided that at home she was an aunt, and at school, she was an ant (spelled aunt). I still use this interchangeably to this day.

There were activities I enjoyed. I joined the Glee Club. I had convinced myself that I had a good singing voice. However, I had difficulty staying on key. I sat in the alto section and was told to stay close to the person next to me and try to follow along. There were times I just had to open my mouth and let nothing come out. But I tried. I found it wasn't difficult adjusting to being in an all-White school as I had been living in an all-white community for a few months. It was a new environment and routine, but I was happy to be at Claymont High.

Besides trying to sing in the Glee Club, I also signed up for softball and basketball, as I enjoyed sports. Basketball was a little difficult because, in those days, girls weren't allowed to use the full court. We had half-court basketball. I usually had to play guard, and that meant staying under the opponent's basket. I rarely had a chance to shoot a basket, probably because the ball wouldn't go into the basket for me. But before I graduated, someone took a picture of me trying to do a layup for the yearbook. Fortunately, it doesn't show that I missed the basket. Of course, women's basketball is totally different today.

Softball was different, and I excelled at it. I was the pitcher for the team. In my first game, I was so nervous, I pitched the first ball over the fence. I cleared everything, including the batter, catcher, and umpire. I settled down, and we won — I think. Maybe I just thought we won. One incident that happened was a White softball team refused to play us. We were very disappointed but consoled ourselves with each other and the staff. We moved on, forgot it, and started preparing for the next game. They did forfeit the game, but we would have liked to have earned the win. It was a reminder to me of the segregation around me. My classmates and staff were great, though, always supportive of me. Again, I have to say that I was happy at Claymont.

In my senior year, we had a new coach. She had a different style. In order to step onto her field, we had to run around the track. In those days, girls didn't run much, especially on the track. After a few days of that, I was exhausted. She grilled us, drilled us, and occassionaly yelled at us. There were times we ran the track again. But we discovered we were winning games. So, we accepted her program.

In fact, we won all of our games, including the state championship. We almost lost our last game. My sister Carol was an outfielder, and the last ball I pitched looked like it was going to sail over her head. But she reached up and backward and caught it with one hand. We all ran and hugged her. High-fives hadn't yet been invented. Thinking about it today, our coach reminded me of some of today's coaches.

All was not over with our softball championship, because the boy's team had a zero championship, having lost all of their games. So, they made the girls' team play them, so they could say they won a game. I was not happy about it and neither was the team. But, we fought hard and didn't lose by much. I had someone slide into me, run over me, and spike me during the game. It was not fun. But I was glad we put up a good showing.

After settling into the Claymont routine, I felt comfortable. I had new friends and enjoyed the many activities. I remember visiting the home of one of my White friends. Her parents were very nice, and that put me at ease.

The big day came when Claymont had to host the Howard High all-Black football team. Everyone knew Claymont would probably lose. Howard's football team was exceptionally good. Everyone, students, and staff, wondered which side of the football field we would sit on. My sisters and I took two minutes to decide.

We entered the stadium that day, walked to the left side where Howard High fans were, waved to those we knew, and continued around to Claymont's side. We felt this was our school now, and we should support it. In fact, all eleven of us Black students sat on the Claymont side, much to the relief of all Claymont High students and staff. Of course, we lost.

We still had relatives in Wilmington, with whom we visited often when we attended the Jack & Jill Club of America, Inc.

It was a good time for me at Claymont High. It was a warm environment, and I had close friends. However, when we left the area for school field trips, I was a little nervous. It reminded me that outside of my new environment, most of the area still embraced segregation. All the field trips were in White communities. I didn't know how the other students would receive me. After a few trips, I realized there were no problems.

There were only three racial incidents at Claymont High. The first being the softball game. The second one involved a White boy taunting my sister Carol. A teacher walked over to the White boy and slapped him really hard. Then the teacher calmly started teaching again, as though nothing had happened. It was instant punishment.

Of course, today you couldn't get away with it. Back in those days, when you returned home and confessed, your mother sided with the teacher. The third incident involved my older sister, Merle. She was in her senior year, and there was a rehearsal for the Baccalaureate service. The girls were supposed to come into the auditorium on one side and the boys on the other. Then they would meet in the center aisle and walk down together.

However, when Merle started down the center aisle, the boy who was supposed to walk with her bolted out of the auditorium. But the boy behind him quickly moved up to take his place. And no one really saw it. But the staff saw it. They had them go down separate aisles at graduation. But at the rehearsals for graduation, they started the students on stage, so there would be no further problems. When they handed out the diplomas, the boy who bolted got a blank one as punishment. Later, they gave him his diploma.

Merle was an excellent piano player and played during the service and received a standing ovation. Her skills always impressed me, and she played exceptionally well that day. It was a very proud moment in my life.

Although my two sisters and I had successfully integrated in Claymont, my other two sisters and brother faced the prospect of being bussed to the Wilmington Elementary School. However, Arden had an elementary school. The Arden School Board of Trustees decided at a special meeting to admit my three siblings.

On September 7, 1952, they officially met and invited them to attend the school. The state of Delaware did not approve, because Arden had not gone through the courts. The cases had applied only to Claymont High School and the Black elementary school in Hockessin. But Arden insisted and finally, after months of discussion, the state allowed the children to remain. Thus, the Arden school became the only one in Delaware to integrate without a lawsuit.

During my first two years at Claymont, there were several events regarding integration. Besides reading, writing, and arithmetic, there were many times we were called to the lawyer's office. They were preparing for the U.S. Supreme Court case. They would ask us how things were going.

I saw it as a constant interruption in my daily activities. I didn't really concern myself with the case because my parents were deeply involved in it. In those days, parents were in charge of the children's activities. I remember when Thurgood Marshall interviewed my mother. I was excited about that. Everyone was. She took a train to Philadelphia to meet with him about the Delaware case.

Later, I discovered the magnitude of the Claymont integration. So, it made sense that we were called into the lawyer's office so often. We were being used as an example of how integration can work. Jack Greenberg argued the case before the U.S. Supreme Court saying that "integration does work because it's been working for two years at Claymont High School."

It became an exciting event since our experience was so peaceful and had been going well for at least four years. It also saddened me that there were negative events in some of the other schools. During my four years at Claymont, school work, glee club, and sports kept me busy. One thing I enjoyed tremendously was being an announcer of local events at a local radio station. I thought I might later study acting. I graduated and was excited to leave high school and pursue college.

My parents were wonderful in providing higher education for us. They expected us to go to college as their generation had done. There was no choice. For this, I am still thankful. Education was always a high value in our family. Most of my father's eleven siblings graduated from college. This was also a time when not too many, especially women, attended college. In fact, there were only two of us from my graduating class who attended college. I had a good upbringing and my parents worked at instilling character. I look back and feel blessed to have them.

CHAPTER 6
COLLEGE YEARS

Fisk University in Nashville, Tennessee.

I decided to attend Fisk University in Nashville, Tennessee, a private, historically Black university in Nashville, Tennessee, founded in 1866. In 1930, Fisk was the first Black institution to be accredited by the Southern Association of Colleges and Schools.

My older sister Merle was starting her third year at Fisk. I didn't want to be alone, so I went there to be near her. I lived in a dormitory, which meant we had hours during which we had to be on campus, but she and her husband had an apartment off campus. Because I was her sister, I had permission to go there. Otherwise, the school rules were that 1st and 2nd year students couldn't leave the campus after a certain time.

I was immediately thrust into deep-South segregation. Fisk was a predominately Black university. There were only a few White exchange students. This was segregation of a kind I had not known. And I did not feel comfortable enough to venture out to other parts of Nashville. Once, some classmates and I went downtown to shop. We stopped in a coffee shop to get something to eat. I sat down at the counter, and I was told to get out. We don't serve you. I was angry and embarrassed, but I couldn't reply. We were told never to answer back.

Another time, we went downtown to what was called an interracial movie theatre. This experience made me never want to go downtown again. We bought our tickets at the front booth, walked down a long, narrow, dimly lit walkway, and ended up in the rear of the building. There was a man to take our tickets. We then walked up 100 steps to the balcony. Someone actually counted them. We sat, but the movie screen was so far away we could barely see or hear. So, we left. As I am writing this, I hear Jesus say, "I was with you protecting you all that time." and "Some of those people you encountered later became Christians and had a change of heart."

I was glad to stay within the confines of the university area. That restriction made me feel safe. But I was confused and frightened because I had not been in this kind of all Black environment before. I felt confined and trapped. But I was still happy to be there. And, there's something about leaving home for the first time, and still having family close by.

I quickly made friends. My roommate and other dormitory ladies were nice. We went to classes and meals together. There were also other activities-concerts and the local Black movie theatre. There were also small local shops and other places we could go to.

I tried out for the basketball team, and in the first tryout, I bombed. These ladies were far superior. I just attended some games instead. I didn't try out for any singing groups as I knew it would be an embarrassment, so I just focused on my studies and visiting my sister.

I was upset at some circumstances of other Black students and what they experienced. My roommate was a pre-med student who was happy to be there and study medicine. After 2 weeks, I came from my classes to find her in tears. She couldn't do her studies. She kept saying, "I was a straight-A student in Florida. I don't understand why I can't do this. I won't be able to be a doctor." She had to change her major to physical education. I really felt bad for her.

I realized my situation was quite different. At Claymont High, I had an excellent education. I remember some teachers were former college professors, who taught on a level that made my learning more difficult, compounded because I was already a slow learner. I was thankful for my parents' help. It raised my grade level, especially in math. At Fisk, I could keep up with all of my classes.

It also showed me that some of the southern high school systems were academically inferior. My roommate wasn't the only one who had to change her major. The law in those days said that the schools had to be separate but equal. They were separate, but some were not equal.

One of the best thing about Fisk was the Fisk Jubilee Singers. They toured the U.S. and Europe, becoming quite a sensation, singing before Ulysses S. Grant, Mark Twain, and Queen Victoria; popularizing spirituals written by Wallace Willis such as "Swing Low Sweet Chariot", and changing racial stereotypes. Fisk is also the home of a music literature collection founded by the noted Harlem Renaissance figure Carl Van Vechten, for whom the campus museum is named. (Wikipedia)

They were magnificent. People from all over the state came to the concerts, leaving standing room only. There was no room for the students inside the building, so we sat on the grass outside. The attendees were paying for tickets, but we weren't. I still have wonderful memories of those concerts. In fact, one of my friends was a backup singer for the group. We were always excited about it.

We had a colorful character there at Fisk. He was the guard on campus, and his job was to protect the students. We called him "WillShoot," because he did shoot his gun. No one knew his real name. It wasn't uncommon to be awakened at night to the sound of gunfire. If we ran to the window, we could see him jumping over bushes, gun in hand. He took his job seriously. My only face-to-face contact with him was when I was walking down the road on campus with another student. Suddenly, he jumped from behind a bush, came up to me, and asked if I was all right. I quickly said "yes", and he disappeared into the bushes again. This took me aback quite a bit, but I glad he was doing his job. He was a favorite conversation topic.

While at Fisk, I took acting classes and had major roles in school plays, which I enjoyed. I had hoped that this would lead to a career in acting. What I realize now is that I should have taken a second major - in math. I got straight A's in Calculus, which I enjoyed. I was young and didn't think too far ahead. It all worked out in the end, though.

These were good years at Fisk because I made friends and pursued an acting career. Also, my sister Merle was graduating, and it looked like I would be in Nashville alone. I felt I had to leave.

This was another frightening time. Something new was difficult to take. Depressions and anger were there. But better times were just ahead. "I know the plans I have for you to give you a good end." Jeremiah 29:11 KJV

Now that they settled the Brown case, it looked like all was continuing to go well for school integration in Delaware. I was watching events from Fisk over the news media. Sadly, it wasn't going too well with many other schools. I couldn't understand why there were so many problems when things went so well with Claymont high. But I recall that at least one White school in lower Delaware had some issues with integration.

But a most spectacular thing happened, which took everyone by surprise. Since there was no Black public high school in lower Delaware, the Black students' education ended when they graduated from 6th grade. White students could attend high school, but many couldn't afford to go to college. Their education ended at the high school level.

When the Brown case settled, both races could get a full education as far as they wanted to go. The White children who couldn't afford to attend college suddenly showed up at the Black state colleges in Delaware and Maryland. They could now get the degree they wanted. I believe that this was the first integration by White students of Black State Colleges. It got no major publicity due to ongoing issues with the other four states involved in the Brown case. Delaware took the lead on integration.

Delaware was the first in many things but especially in education integration. We showed the world that all races could and can live and work together to achieve not only integration but also harmony. God's love can do this if we are willing.

CHAPTER 7
SALVATION AT
BOSTON
UNIVERSITY

I decided after two years at Fisk University in Nashville, Tennessee that I would pursue an acting career. Since my sister Carol was on scholarship at the Boston Conservatory of Music, I chose to start my new career in Boston. But at first, I couldn't decide if I should go. So, I flipped a coin. It came out Fisk. Carol, not liking the outcome, snatched the coin and flipped it again. That flip turned out to be Boston University. So, we ignored the first flip.

Boston University

Moving to Boston was extraordinarily beautiful and felt like a breath of fresh air. It felt like I had a new lease on life. I was moving further away from home than when I was at Fisk University and was transferring to BU while embarking on my acting career. At Fisk, I discovered my acting talents and having my sister Carol in Boston made my life easier. We spent some time together, meeting each others' friends and enjoying activities.

I enjoyed the city life - mainly classical concerts, of which my sister played in many. There were also pre-Broadway theatre productions. It was nice seeing them before they hit Broadway. My classmates and I felt privileged to be among the first to see them.

Walking around Boston was a treat with all the shops, restaurants, and museums. Well-kept green grass and tall trees lined the waterways. While I was living in Boston, I relished learning the history of such a famous city. When you are on Boston Common, you can almost hear the echoes of the American Revolution.

One of the places I most enjoyed was the Boston Common, which was founded in 1634 and was the location of many significant historical events. It is where the Colonial militia mustered for the start of the Revolutionary War. From 1760 to 1768, the Redcoats staged an eight-year occupation and intimidated and harassed the public which may have contributed to the discontent of the people. Many of our great leaders like George Washington, John Adams, and General Lafayette gathered there to celebrate our nation's independence. In the 1860s, Civil War recruitment and anti-slavery meetings were held on the Common.

During World War I, when food was scarce, the locals planted victory gardens. Then for World War II, when the nation was building the war machine, the Common donated most of its iron fencing for scrap metal.

Boston Common lives on vibrantly as a stage for free speech and public assembly, including speeches and events by such notables as Charles Lindbergh who held a crowd mesmerized with his promotion of commercial aviation. It was also one of the many sites where anti-Vietnam War protests and civil rights rallies took place, including one held by Martin Luther King, Jr. Also in 1979, Pope John Paul II celebrated Mass on the Common.

As I wandered around the city, I found myself in the very spot where the Boston Tea Party occurred. The Boston Tea Party was an American political and mercantile protest by the Sons of Liberty in Boston, Massachusetts, on December 16, 1773. The citizens were tired of paying hefty, unjust taxes. A group of colonists dressed as Native Americans and rebelled by tossing crates of tea overboard into the harbor. It was a prelude to war. It was thrilling to stand on the very cobblestones and visit the places that our founding fathers stood upon to announce our independence from England.

There were so many things to see and enjoy. I started to really love living in Boston. I even attended some BU ball games. They were not good at football, having lost so many games. They eventually canceled the entire program. Many students were very upset about it, especially those that had football scholarships. Their careers would end if they couldn't find another school to attend. The school focused on hockey, where they excelled.

BU was huge with 25,000 students. The university had grown to where there weren't enough women's dormitories. They bought some residential buildings. I lived in one of them. It was interesting because other tenants refused to move out. It worked for the student's benefit because we became close enough to the other tenants to babysit occasionally for their children and earn pocket change. We became a vital part of their community-like family.

For someone from the tiny state of Delaware, and the small campus at Fisk, the enormity of BU was almost overwhelming. It had a small Black population and was difficult to connect with them. After I met some, we got together for social events. I was now in an almost White environment. It didn't bother me because I had been in several similar environments previously. This was nothing new. I had friends from both races. Schoolwork was a little hard, and I had to juggle classwork with theatre work.

My primary focus was schoolwork and theatre productions. With only two years to go until my graduation, I focused on productions and attending acting classes. It was very good being a part of the theatre group. They became my close friends. We would go out together to the local restaurant and bar. Most of my classes at BU were in theatre. These were exciting times.

My life had changed for the good. But there were still those nagging bouts of depression, anger, loneliness, and my temper still flared. I felt better when I was alone. I sometimes cried, and there were times when I was not too nice toward others.

However, Jesus was changing things for me. "I will not forget you."

In the residential building, there were five of us living in one apartment with two bedrooms. When I arrived, three of my roommates had already taken the large one. That left me with the smaller one with Beatrice. There was something different about her. The other three and I talked about her. She was always praying and reading her Bible. We thought it was a little strange, especially since she wouldn't socialize with us. She was very nice, though, and we got along well together. She was really a good roommate.

One of my roommates had a car. She let us use it when we needed it. Once we drove down to New York to sightsee and meet other friends. It was a short trip, but having a car made it even more fun. We enjoyed riding around. We probably overused the car. Another time, the girl who owned the car drove us to New York to stay with her parents. They were very nice and fed us well. They had a beautiful house and property.

There was so much to see and do while in Boston. I decided right after I arrived I was going to live there always. I especially enjoyed the long walks and beautiful scenery. Boston was truly a wonderful city.

Beatrice started talking to me about Jesus. I started listening, nd I realized that I was missing something. I needed a higher being to help me with my problems and issues. The BIG day finally arrived when Beatrice led me in a prayer for salvation. "If you shall confess with your mouth the Lord Jesus, and believe in your heart that God raised him from the dead, you shall be saved." Romans 10:9-11 KJV

I asked Jesus to come into my heart and be my Savior. He came in and I immediately felt a huge weight lift off my shoulders. It was like being flooded with the depths of His love, mercy, and grace, and being cleansed of all sin. I felt at peace. One of the most spectacular things was that my temper disappeared. To this day, it has never returned.

I felt light and beautiful. I could look at myself in the mirror and see a beautiful child of God. Overwhelmed with His love, it was easier for me to tolerate people and situations. I was excited. When I went outside, everything came alive - the sky, trees, and flowers vibrated with more vivid color. I was now a born-again Christian and happy to be one. "In the same way, I tell you, there is joy in the presence of the angels of God over one sinner who repents." Luke 15:10 KJV

Beatrice gave me a Bible. At first, I didn't know what to do with it. But, suddenly, a bible study started in our room. It was interesting, and I learned who Jesus was to me and how much He loved and cared about me. We continued these Bible studies until graduation. My relationship with Beatrice grew, and I also grew as a Christian.

During those two years, my destiny seemed to be in Boston, as I continued to grow in Him. He was the reason I was led to Boston—to know and grow in the Lord. I often reflect on the coin toss.

I also learned to tithe. I resisted it because my allowance only lasted through the third week of the month. I usually had to borrow money to make it to the next paycheck. I didn't see how I could do it. I was grateful for what my father sent me, but it wasn't enough. So, I obeyed and gave my tithe. Miracle upon miracle, I ended up with money left over at the end of the month. I had never seen a miracle like this before. I believe that this was one of my first since becoming a Christian. Later, my father realized I needed more money and increased my allowance. "Bring ye all the tithes into the storehouse, that there may be meat in mine house, and prove me now herewith, saith the LORD of hosts, if I will not open you the windows of heaven, and pour you out a blessing, that there shall not be room enough to receive it." Malachi 3:10 KJV.

There were many great things that happened during those years. For the first time, I came to know that Someone really big loved me. I was thrilled and content. I could look back now and see God standing over my crib, carefully watching over me and protecting and caring for me. I felt like I was in Heaven.

His Word says, "His love is beyond measure." Romans 8:38-39. I was so excited that I was born again.

Those of us who were Christians attended Harold Ockanga's Church. I enjoyed going there. We studied our Bibles and grew in knowledge of Him. One day, the pastor showed up at one of our young people's fellowships and gave us support. I loved that church and my new friends.

I wanted to stay in Boston. It was now June of 1960. Those two years went by quickly. It was time for my graduation. My parents flew up to Boston for the big event. It was their first time in Boston, and we all dined out in one of those fancy, delicious restaurants. With six kids in the family, it was very special that they made the trip for me. They were wonderful parents. The next day, they departed for Delaware. I knew they would be back next year for Carol's graduation.

At BU, I was happy with my B- average, which was a miracle because I was a slow learner. I had difficulty figuring things out. I had tutors in High School. This helped tremendously, because I learned math, which became my best class at Fisk University. I earned an A on my final exam in calculus. Today, I think about it, and wish I had pursued more studies in math in addition to acting. But down the road, I used my math while working in the finance departments of companies, like the AICPA and Landor.

Sadly, I had to leave Boston. Not knowing what to do or where to go, I consulted with my parents. They told me I could come back to their new home in Delaware. I packed my bags, said my goodbyes, and headed back home.

My parent's house was now in Ardencroft, Delaware. I moved there to decide what to do next. It was strange having completed all of my education. Part of me was frightened. The years had gone by so fast. I kept thinking, what do I do now? There was nothing in the acting field in Delaware. My major at BU was theatre education, with a minor in public speaking. There were no jobs in those fields. I realized later that I should have picked a major where I could get a job. No one advised me on this in school.

When I arrived home, my Mother pulled me aside and told me the truth - that she had raised me on the advice from a doctor's book. It said "Don't show love to your newborn. Only pick them up to feed them and change their diapers." I lived this way for the first year of my life. At that time, parents were told this was the right thing to do.

I still remember the pain and anguish she felt in telling me this. She carried this around in her heart for 22 years. She continued the story by telling me that the next year, the doctors realized and confessed they had made a mistake and that a mother should love, touch and cuddle her children from birth onward. Shocked to hear this, I didn't know what to say. I thought this might be why I had so many problems. Of the six children my parents had, I was the only one raised like this.

Soon, a friend I met previously offered to let me stay in her parent's house with her in Philadelphia. At least I would be closer to where I could pursue an acting career. It would mean packing again. I really didn't want to stay at home. There's something about moving on. My siblings were also moving on in their careers in other places.

I prayed and asked the Lord what to do next. The answer was to continue to pursue an acting career. So, I moved to Ardmore, Pennsylvania, and lived with my friend and her family. I got a job as a clerk typist in an organization called Scripture Union and started attending the Philadelphia Academy of Acting. I learned a lot and was excited about getting acting jobs.

My spiritual life continued to grow. I met new friends and attended church regularly. But there were still those nagging depressions, fears, anxieties, and anger. I no longer had the temper tantrums, but I still withdrew and sometimes faked my way through work and social events.

In addition to my talk with my mother, I began further to understand my problems when I worked in a hospital for emotionally disturbed children. Seeing the children and their issues, I realized I also had problems and issues. So, I saw a psychiatrist who helped me to understand some things - like the impact of my treatment as a child, and I felt better. I didn't see him for very long, because I was moving away.

So, I prayed again and believed Jesus wanted me to pursue an acting career. I would have to move to New York. I really wanted to go back to Boston. But deep down inside, I knew I should go to New York. So, I packed my bags again and moved on. I had happy times in Pennsylvania with my friends. We attended concerts, ballgames, movies, and church outings.

I was a new person in Christ Jesus. 2 Corinthians 5:17 ESV "Therefore, if anyone is in Christ, he is a new creation. The old has passed away; behold, the new has come." There were times I felt His peace – peace like a river. I was learning how to walk with Him. I was still taking baby steeps. I knew he loved me.

Those earlier years at BU were now very special because that's where I met my Savior. "For God so loved the world that he gave his one and only Son, that whoever believes in him shall not perish but have eternal life." John 3:16 NIV. It was almost like a child waking up on Christmas morning and seeing a big box with a beautiful bow. I could only imagine it being what I wanted and hugged it, played with it and immensely enjoyed it.

Jesus was with me wherever I had been and wherever I would go. His love is unconditional.

But even though things were going well in my Christian life, I continued to live in my hidden world.

Chapter 8 How to Succeed in Business Without Really Trying

I made it! I had attained my Bachelor's Degree, and I had a feeling that things would go well after graduation with my dreams of a successful acting career.

But how would I get there? Where would I live? I had no job. How would I support myself? I had heard of so many actors, coming to New York with nothing, and not making it. They had to go back home. I needed the Lord's help. I had learned to pray and read my Bible, which I did. I still felt a desire to move to New York. I asked a Christian friend from Pennsylvania who was now living in New York if I could come to visit for two weeks so I could look for a job and an apartment. She said yes.

I packed yet again, took a train to New York, then a cab to her place. The taxi driver gave me the scenic ride. It was expensive, but I enjoyed it so much that I was already falling in love with New York.

Part of the taxi ride went through the park, and I decided I would, one day, take the horse and carriage ride through Central Park, which I did. There were paths for people, cars, and horses amidst beautiful scenery, tall trees, shimmering ponds and lots of people. It was the place to visit. Like an oasis in the middle of a desert, Central Park was constructed and designed in the mid-1800s, and is the most popular park in the world. Smack in the middle of upper Manhattan, it provides a much-needed, beautiful and peaceful refuge for city dwellers. In fact, as of 2016, 42 million people had visited the park. (Wikipedia)

Central Park, New York City

My friends and I loved to stroll the paths and lie in the grass dreaming of the future. There are so many wonderful attractions - lovely landscapes such as the Ramble and Lake, Hallett Nature Sanctuary, the Jacqueline Kennedy Onassis Reservoir, and Sheep Meadow. There is entertainment at the Wollman Ice Rink, Central Park Carousel, and the Central Park Zoo. There are also more formal features such as the Central Park Mall and Bethesda Terrace; and the Delacorte Theater.

Visitors love the horse-drawn carriages and bicycle tours, cycling, sports facilities, and concerts and events such as Shakespeare in the Park. Central Park has various roads and paths which public transportation can access. It's a model for the world's urban parks. The first place I visited was the Empire State Building, which reaches 102 stories into the sky. It is a lovely art deco skyscraper in Midtown Manhattan. As of 2022, the building is the seventh tallest building in New York City, the ninth tallest completed skyscraper in the United States, the 54th tallest in the world, and the sixth tallest freestanding structure in the Americas.

Every year, around four million tourists from around the world visit the building's 86th and 102nd-floor observatories. An additional indoor observatory on the 80th floor opened in 2019. The Empire State Building is an international cultural icon: it has been featured in more than 250 television series and films since the movie King Kong was released in 1933. The building's size has become the global standard of reference to describe the height and length of other structures.

Another fun experience is riding the ferries. Water surrounds Manhattan on all sides. Eventually, I was sure that one day I would be taking a ferry to work or just for pleasure. These would be exciting trips, viewing the skylines, taking in the fresh air, sometimes with a light mist. I could see people embarking on them and settling down for a beautiful scenic trip. This was going to be a fun place to live.

I was totally unprepared for the New York apartment where I stayed. I had grown up in a nice, big house with lots of rooms and a big, beautiful yard, garden, and playground. What was this? They called it a "railroad apartment." It was long and extremely narrow. There was a tiny kitchen, bath, and bedroom. I think I slept on the floor. No, now I remember. She had a tiny couch where I slept. But the most bizarre thing was the many locks on the door. What was this place? Apparently, there was crime here? I had never heard of or seen anything like it in Delaware. And the roach and rodent population was unreal. We had mice in Delaware, which we thought our small dog would eliminate. We were wrong. The silly little mice scared him, and he ran toward us each time he saw one. I wondered as I looked around this dingy apartment, *Is this the place Jesus wants me to be*? That question would soon be answered.

My first plan was to get a job. I looked in newspapers and got suggestions from my temporary roommate. I got a job almost immediately, working as a clerk typist for McCall's Magazine company. What a miracle. I could move to New York, start working, and then look for acting jobs. This to me was just like "How to succeed in Business Without Really Trying." I call it (HSB-WORT).

While there on my trip, I put in an application to live in a women's residence. New York was full of them. They were inexpensive and included meals and utilities. Subway and bus transportation were also cheap – 15 cents. I felt I could afford to live there, and I was excited. My friend agreed to let me stay in her apartment until I had my own place. So, I went home to Delaware and packed all of my meager belongings. I had learned to pack light.

During my first weekend living in New York, someone told me about a church I could attend. So, I went to the Sunday service at Madison Avenue Presbyterian Church. After the service, I somehow met the Pastor and his wife. They immediately invited me to stay with them until the residence where I would live was ready. Their apartment was on 5th Avenue, overlooking Central Park - spectacular views. They let me stay for free. I thought, *It doesn't get any better than this*. (HSB-WORT).

I came to know the doorman. I wish I remembered his name. We were both sports addicts, and always talked excitedly about the local teams, especially when they won. The only thing about him was that he kept referring to me as the maid. I could never make him understand I wasn't the maid. I remember the day I yelled at him and upset him greatly. I felt bad, and later I realized it wasn't his fault. He grew up in an era when, if you were Black, you were probably a maid.

I decided to keep the friendship and accept him as he was. The time came when a residence opened up, and it was time to move again. I told the doorman I was moving to another place. We were both upset about the possibility of never seeing each other again. I still remember him fondly.

I also spent time sightseeing, amazed at the tall buildings and all the museums. Metropolitan Museum was my favorite. There were so many different exhibits. I knew how I wanted to spend my days off. There was so much to see and do. I couldn't wait to get started. Years later, when my mother would come to visit, she always wanted to see the museums. I think we saw them all - not really, but it seemed so. As of 2022, there are approximately 145 of them. One of my favorites was 'Lady in Gold.' I saw the film and was excited to see the original photos in New York City. They were spectacular.

To get my resume in order, I had photos taken for my portfolio and started making the rounds. There wasn't that much on my resume because I hadn't had many acting jobs. I had gotten some small parts in summer theatre where I only had one-liners. There were also roles in a few plays in college. That was it. I wondered how I might get any acting jobs. So, I prayed and read my Bible.

I started going to agencies and leaving my resume. Soon, I got a call for an interview. I was excited but didn't want to get my hopes up. In the back of my mind, I thought of all the aspiring actors who didn't make it. I met some of them and really felt bad as I watched them tearfully leave town.

Joan during her acting career.

Within a few days, I had an acting job on the daytime soap opera, "Search for Tomorrow." (HSB-WORT). I was told the reason I got a job so easily was because the door for Black actresses on soap operas had just opened. I walked right through it. Many top actors got their start on "Search for Tomorrow." It was 1967.

A little later, I got a job on another soap opera, "Another World." I gave glory to Jesus for these spectacular miracles. I was on both shows concurrently but on different days. Fortunately, there was no conflict. It was absolutely thrilling to be fulfilling my dream.

Each day was beautiful. My soap opera days started early. The shows were only 15 minutes, and they were live. So, I could keep my clerical job in the afternoon. I enjoyed getting to know the other actors and witnessed to some of them about Jesus. I gave a book about Old Testament times to those who wanted it. Many did. I experienced great success in my acting career and met many celebrities. Mary Stewart, the main character of "Search for Tomorrow", stands out in my memory.

I was a star in soap operas, since I was the first Black actress. I enjoyed immensely my new life in the limelight. To my surprise, I even got some mail from fans. Life was so very good, and I praised Jesus for the miracles. I also took some acting classes and met many other actors. Little did I know that one of them would give me the title for this chapter.

It happened one day when I was walking down the street, and I spotted him and walked over to see him. We chatted and suddenly, I heard "ACTION." I was in the middle of a movie scene! So, I continued to walk down the sidewalk with the other actors. When we got to the street, I went my way.

The title of the movie was "How to Succeed in Business Without Really Trying." An appropriate title that reflected how easily success in New York had come. Life with Jesus can be fun and miraculous! My success was going to my head. After only two years, the celebrity status consumed me. It had gotten a hold of me. I dreamed of being rich and famous with people looking up to me and me looking down on them.

So, one day while in prayer, I heard Jesus say to me "Leave the acting career. I have something else for you to do." It was a very hard decision because I could feel that "monkey", but I said yes. More job offers came in; I turned them down. People would ask me why I was leaving. I really didn't know what to tell them. To the Christians, I would say that Jesus told me to.

Then one day, I knelt in prayer and asked Jesus, WHY? He said, "If you had kept going the way you were, you would have left me." I was shocked to hear that. I didn't think I could ever do that. But I knew I had that "monkey" and after I said yes, it left me. I know now that I needed a deeper walk with Jesus. I still needed healing and to experience His deep love for me. And that's what I did. I moved on.

There was nothing wrong with me being an actress. It was the control it was having over me. I had somewhat stopped working to overcome depression, fears, oppressions. I seemed to want to do things my way, which was not the way of Jesus - the way of loving Him, loving my neighbor, and being kind. It was necessary that I accept myself and show unconditional love and forgiveness to others.

My next journey took me to Teen Challenge. It was a Christian drug rehabilitation center run by David Wilkerson. It was life in the raw since we went to the streets to minister to addicts and offer to take them home with us. Some wanted to get clean and came with us. The painful part was their withdrawal from drugs. It was cold turkey, and we stayed up with them for about 24 hours. We prayed and encouraged them with Bible verses. Some days, it was around the clock. They all came out of it. For only one did we have to call an ambulance, but she made it.

There was a day when I needed to find another job. I had just lost one, and the rent was due. I only had $50.00 left. I went to church, and during the service, Jesus spoke to me and told me to put the $50.00 in the collection. I argued it was all I had, and I would have to walk home, and there wouldn't be money for dinner and the weekend, and the rent was due next Friday.

But I put it in the offering. I started walking home a little angry, but when I arrived I wasn't tired. When I got inside my building, I saw a note, a free meal tonight. I thought, this is great, I can make it until tomorrow. Then the phone rang. And a friend invited me to stay with their family for the weekend. I was happy to accept. So I had free meals all weekend. When they drove me back to New York, one handed me $50.00.

This was Monday. I went for an interview on Tuesday, got the job and started working right away, and had enough to pay rent.

When I looked at what had happened, I realized that if I had not put the $50 in the offering, I would have gotten home too soon and missed the call. I would have fed my face and gone looking for a job on Monday. But the job was not available until Tuesday. It amazes me the way Jesus provides if you trust him.

A footnote to this is that in the same service was a young man who had an argument with Jesus when he asked him to put his last $10.00 in the offering. He told us the next week that he had refused. He walked out of church, went two blocks, and was robbed of the $10.00. I was thinking later that had he put it in the offering, Jesus would have provided another way home for him.

There were more miracles, especially those when Jesus healed me from my past, not only from fears and anger but also from stubbornness. I remember, as a young person, when I had an argument over a pair of pajamas with one of my sisters. We each said they were ours. I finally realized that they really were hers, but I was too stubborn to give up the argument. I ended up sleeping in her smelly PJs.

Some of the most wonderful miracles were when Jesus gave me friends in New York. I had only been living In New York for a short time when I met Joyce and Carol in church. They both had and still do have a prophetic ministry. Later, I met Norma, and she also became a true friend. These three became my lifelong friends. Healing miracles began to take place, as they prayed and gave me words from Jesus. The truly miraculous healing that began for me as a lonely baby, continued for many years.

I didn't really realize how deep was the anguish within me, but today I can finally say that I am completely healed. Jesus truly is a miracle-working friend.

CHAPTER 9 ESCAPE FROM THE COOKIE MONSTER

I have lived in a great place all of my adult life — and that place is New York City.

I've had an illustrious career in acting, worked in Teen Challenge, a drug rehab center, and enjoyed a career in finance for the American Institute of Certified Public Accountants. I am currently retired from Landor, the world's largest specialist brand and design group. I enjoy working there among such talented people. Also, my Company sent a donation to UNCEF on my behalf for the work done on the Brown case. Our parent company sent a match. Some of my co-workers have been helping me with this book. For example, our professional photographer took the cover picture.

Jesus has gifted me with a love for people. I am no longer completely self-absorbed. With the help of my friends and ministries, I have overcome past obstacles, and I continue to grow in Jesus. I credit my dear friends, Joyce, Carol and Norma, because of their prophetic God-given words to me. They could see right through me and point out when I was faking it. Then I would repent and ask for help in changing. Repentance and forgiveness were the key. I knew I wanted a deeper walk with Jesus. To this day, I still ask Him if there is anything I need to change. I choose to yield all to Him and to receive His ways of living. So, the other key is obedience. The word says it is better than sacrifice. It leads to a healthy and prosperous life.

Growth has been a constant years-long healing process with a great deal of help from others. I attend a wonderful church - Faith Exchange Fellowship, where there really is fellowship in Jesus and loving relationships. "Forsake not the assembling of yourselves together." Hebrews 10:25-31 KJV. Dan and Annie Stratton, our pastors, have a prophetic and teaching ministry, helping us to grow in Jesus. I am always blessed in the services with their messages. Pastor Dan reminds us we are destined for greatness, but we can't do it alone. He also says, "We win! Let's play."

The Pastors opened their hearts to us and always have time for us, no matter what. They have started an intercessory prayer group, of which I am a part. We get our prayers answered with miracles. The love of Jesus/Yeshua is strong in them and also in the congregation.

I love to attend church every week. The messages and the bonding of the body of Christ give me the power to overcome all obstacles. I no longer stay within myself. In times past, I sometimes simply waved goodbye and quickly left when the service ended, but now I participate in the faith community.

I am so very thankful for my church, Faith Exchange. Jesus knows just the right place for me to love and be loved. I am dedicated to staying in the Word and in prayer. And most of all, I'm learning to pay it forward, helping others. I also have family members in Tennessee with whom I fellowship. "I will provide for all of your needs," Philippians 4:19 KJV, and I know this extends even to family fellowship.

It feels good to be set free from the bondage of isolation and depression. And I praise my savior for my healings. He doesn't just leave us where we are with no hope. "... he will also provide the way of escape, that you may be able to endure it." (1 Corinthians 10:13 NKJV)

His word also says he heals us. "He sent His word and healed them and delivered them from their destructions." Psalm 107 NKJV, and "Beloved, I pray that you may prosper in all things and be in health just as your soul prospers." 3 John 2 NKJV

It seems like it took a long time to overcome past struggles, but with a lot of help and my willingness to be set free, it finally happened. Life is exciting these days. I forgave and forgot the past and knew it was time to move on. I still pray for that deeper walk with Jesus that will continue to help me grow in Him.

There was that instance which I call "Escape from the Cookie Monster." Well, how did I know I had a major problem with a cookie? I was an adult woman, after all. It was only one cookie. And I didn't care for sweets. Really? Well, I have to be honest. I had a stash of them. I had to have them. Sometimes they consumed my thoughts. I panicked when the store ran out! I remember when I saw that evangelist on TV who had the SAME problem as me. I thought, we're both in trouble.

Then Yeshua showed me a picture of Him and me having a conversation and a cookie came between us. What did I do? I snatched it and ate it. And

He said to me, "You missed part of what I was saying." I repented, and with mixed emotions, gave up that delicious cookie. No more— - forever and forever. God help me. And He did. He then said to me, if the revenge of the cookie monster attacks, what will you do? I said I'm delivered and will remember the scripture, "Thou shalt have no other gods before me." Exodus 20:3 KJV. I rejoiced at being delivered from bouts of missing what Jesus was saying to me. It was a small cookie but a big miracle. I thank Him for helping me. He is such a good Abba Father.

CHAPTER 10
MOM'S FAMILY

My story is only one part of a greater story of my family—many of those who came before have also fought for freedom from their past. I'd like to tell you about two ancestors who inspired me on my journey, etc. All the members of my family have been very special to me, but especially my great, great Uncle Alexander Walters who became the head bishop of the African Methodist Episcopal Church (AME) in America. He was also one of the top civil rights leaders in America. I am happy that he wrote his autobiography, "My Life and Work," so that all could read about his life and times. That book was an inspiration to me as I began to tell my own story.

He was my mother's great-uncle. Julia Waters, his niece, was my mother's mother. Below is a handwritten note that he wrote to my grandmother. It reads "To Julia Walters from her Uncle Bishop Alexander Walters." My family has a copy of the original book he wrote in 1916, which was republished in 2016.

To Julia Walters
From her Uncle
Bishop Alexander
Walters

Alexander was born in 1858 into slavery. His parents and siblings were slaves to their master, Michael Donohue, and his wife, both of whom treated them well. However, an event took place that angered his master who then sent Alexander's mother to be traded to another family. In the book, he states that the Negro slave traders, who brought the slaves to America, set up an auction to trade her to another White slave owner. This was how the slave market worked.

Everyone in his master's house was very upset, including the master's wife. She pleaded for her return, telling him that Alexander's mother was her slave from her youth. The master changed his mind and brought his mother back. Undoubtedly, there was rejoicing. I look back and think my family had divine protection. Jesus knew his future and kept his mother from harm.

Alexander was 6-years-old when slavery was abolished.

Growing up, he excelled in school, entered seminary and ultimately became a bishop. He was very concerned about the plight of the Negro, still enslaved in many ways. He knew that even though physical slavery was abolished, social and political slavery continued.

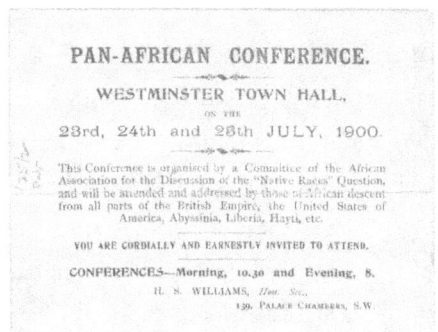

PAN-AFRICAN CONFERENCE.

WESTMINSTER TOWN HALL,

ON THE

23rd, 24th and 25th JULY, 1900.

This Conference is organised by a Committee of the African Association for the Discussion of the "Native Races" Question, and will be attended and addressed by those of African descent from all parts of the British Empire, the United States of America, Abyssinia, Liberia, Hayti, etc.

YOU ARE CORDIALLY AND EARNESTLY INVITED TO ATTEND.

CONFERENCES—Morning, 10.30 and Evening, 8.

H. S. WILLIAMS, Hon. Sec.,
139, PALACE CHAMBERS, S.W.

ALEXANDER WALTERS.

Becoming a bishop at 30 years of age, he was the youngest one ever. He set about changing the laws, holding many conferences in the planning of how to accomplish it. He constantly called people to non-violent action. He chose to take his grievances to Congress rather than the streets. Once he became head bishop, his conferences started with prayer and ended with prayer. Many of the "who's who" in the civil rights movement came to his conferences. He became famous for his approach to civil rights, avoiding the route of marches, rallies, or violent confrontations. Instead, he went straight to the legislators, senators, congressmen, lawmakers, and the White House. In his earlier years, he felt more could have been done by the government, but later he credits Abraham Lincoln with abolishing slavery.

He was eloquent of speech with remarkable writing skills. President Woodrow Wilson offered him an ambassadorship to Liberia, which he declined. He was too busy trying to change the plight of the Negro. There's a handwritten letter from the president in his book in which he declines an invitation by the bishop to attend an event. President Wilson, by executive order and through the influence of Judge Robert Hudspeth, gave the Bishop an appointment to a clerkship at Ellis Island.

He was extremely well-known and always presented his cases with intelligence and the power of prayer. He always prayed, read his Bible, and said, "The solution to the race problems is Jesus Christ." He traveled the world. He loved England, probably because the Negro was well-accepted there. Most of all, he loved Israel which had not yet become a nation and described it beautifully. He was excited about that trip. It was the birthplace of Jesus, and he described it beautifully in his book. Here is the excerpt from his book where he describes his visit to Israel:

From Cairo we returned to Alexandria and took ship for Joppa. After two days' sail we landed at the port. It was here that Jonah shipped for Tarshish when commanded by the Lord to go to Nineveh, and subsequently had trouble with the whale. Here the timbers were landed which had been cut in the mountains of Lebanon to build Solomon's Temple. In this city Peter, while in a trance upon the housetop, beheld a sheet let down from heaven containing all manner of four-footed beasts of the earth, and creeping things, and fowls of the air; and there came to him a voice saying: "Arise, Peter, kill and eat." And Peter said: "Not so, Lord, for I have never eaten anything that is common or unclean." The voice spoke unto him again, the second time: "What God hath cleansed, that call not thou common." This convinced Peter.

Here Dorcas was raised to life. Here I slept on a housetop, in imitation of what Peter had done. The city is built on the side of a hill. The most of the houses are stone, with earthen floors and flat roofs in the old oriental style. There are some beautiful lemon groves about Joppa. The bazaars are very good, but not as fine as in other cities.

After visiting other places of interest in Joppa we left for Jerusalem, which is about thirty-five miles distant. The first place of note on leaving Joppa is the Plain of Sharon, which extends from Jaffa to Cesarea. This is the Plain in which the lilies grew of which Jesus spoke. The next place is Ramleh, a village of four or five thousand inhabitants. There is a great tower near the town, and from this tower can be obtained a fine view of the Plain of Sharon, as far down as Askalon, and as far up as Mount Carmel.

Next comes the Valley of Ajalon. This valley was made famous by the battle which Joshua had with the kings. He prayed that the sun might stand still over Gibeon and the moon be stayed in the Valley of Ajalon, until he obtained the victory over his enemies.

From here we entered Koloneih; along by it runs the ravine out of which David gathered the stones with which to slay Goliath.

I imagined I could see him as he left the armies of Saul and descended the valley with God in his view, trusting in Him for help.

We turned our steps next toward Emmaus, which is on a descent just before you come in sight of Jerusalem. This is the village where Christ went with His disciples on the day of the Resurrection, and reasoned with them by the way; and when He had left them they said: "Did not our hearts burn within us as He talked with us?"

A short while after leaving here we came in sight of Jerusalem. We entered on the western side, along which runs the Valley of Gihon. We entered through the Jaffa Gate; near this gate stands the old tower of David. We passed down David Street, which is very narrow, not more than eight or ten feet wide. Camels and donkeys and the bazaars are all crowded in and along this street. We passed down into Christian Street, and before long reached the church of the Holy Sepulchre.

This is a large and spacious building containing a great many chapels. The Greeks, Latins, Armenians, Copts, Abyssinians, all have chapels under this roof. The first object shown us was the Stone of Unction. When the body of Jesus was taken down from the cross, it was laid upon the Stone for anointing. Lamps hang over and surround the stone. Under the dome, in the centre of the church, is the Holy Sepulchre; it lies within a small chapel, 26 by 18 feet, and built of marble. The hole of the Sepulchre is round, it being cut in the side of the rock. The Sepulchre, itself, is only six by seven feet. The vestibule of the chapel called the Angels' Chapel contains the stone which the angels rolled away from the mouth of the tomb. Just at the back of the Sepulchre is the Chapel of the Copts. North of the Sepulchre is an open court, where Jesus said to Mary, "Woman, why weepest thou"? Many are the sacred places round about and in the church of the Holy Sepulchre; notably the Hill of Calvary, the rent which was made in the stone on the day of Christ's death.

We next visited the Pool of Bethesda. There is no water in the Pool now, and excavations have well nigh destroyed its beauty. There is a little stream issuing from the Pool of Siloam. The Mosque of Omar is a place of great interest. It is built on Mt. Moriah, the spot where the old temple stood which was built by Solomon. The Mosque is surrounded by a wall 1601 feet long on the west; 1530 feet on the east; 1024 feet on the north, and 922 feet on the south. It is entered by eight gates on the west. The Jews' Wailing Place is at the old wall and is said to have been built by David. There are seven gates to the City of Jerusalem: the Jaffa Gate, Damascus Gate, St. Stephen's Gate, Dung Gate, Zion Gate, Golden Gate and Gate of Herod.

It is about two and a half miles around the walls; the walls are from 32 to 42 feet in height, and in some places 15 feet thick. On the east side of the city is the Valley of Jehoshaphat; on the south side is the Valley of Himmon. Just across this Valley is the Garden of Gethsemane; it was in this Garden that Christ was apprehended after His wonderful agony and prayer.

From Gethsemane we visited the Mount of Olives, called also Mt. Olivet. It is an inconsiderable ridge lying on the east side of Jerusalem, made famous by the ascent of the Master, from its peak in the heaven.

There is a minaret on the summit of the mountain from the top of which is one of the grandest views imaginable. Stretched at your feet is the Garden of Gethsemane and the city of Jerusalem; a little in the distance, looking toward the south, is the River Jordan and the Dead Sea. The top of Mount Carmel is seen in the west, while Bethlehem lies to the southeast.

To Bethlehem, which is about six miles from Jerusalem, we next directed our way. Just before entering the city, we came to Rachel's tomb; it is without the City gate. This is where Jacob buried his beloved wife, Rachel. Soon after leaving Rachel's tomb, we entered Bethlehem, the birthplace of our blessed Saviour, and of our King David. It is a small walled town of four or five thousand inhabitants. The Church of the Nativity covers the grotto where Christ was born. Like the Holy Sepulchre at Jerusalem, it is subdivided among the Greeks, Armenians, Latins, etc. A silver star marked the spot where Christ was born. The manger stands in a low recess cut from the rock, a few feet from this star.

Other places of interest in the grotto are the chapel and tomb of St. Jerome; the well renowned for the libation which David poured out of water which had been gotten by a daring exploit by three of his mighty men, on hearing him exclaim: "O, that one would give me drink of the water of the well of Bethlehem, which is by the gate!" When it was brought he poured it out as a libation to the Lord, saying: "Be it far from me, O Lord, that I should do this. Is not this the blood of the men that went by jeopardy of their lives?" Therefore he would not drink of it.

Here the angels appeared unto the shepherds, telling them of the birth of Jesus, and sang an anthem in honor of the new born King. Herethe wise men brought their gifts of gold, frankincense and myrrh, and laid them at the feet of the infant Sovereign. Over this city the star appeared which guided the wise men to the spot where the young child was born.

From Bethlehem we directed our course to Hebron, one of the oldest cities in the Land of Palestine, the home of Abraham and

Jacob. It is in the cave of Macpelah that Abraham buried his beloved wife Sarah. It is now a Mosque, in possession of the Mohammedans. Not a great distance from Hebron is the Valley of Eschol, where the spies from the camp of Israel gathered grapes to carry back to Moses as a sample of the fruit of the land. The bunches were so large that they had to be borne on a pole between two men. I had the pleasure of eating grapes in this valley, which I considered a great privilege. From Hebron we returned to Bethlehem. The next route lay from there to Marsaba, which is a convent in the midst of grand scenery, utterly barren and desolate. It is a gigantic structure, built in terraces into a kind of amphitheatre on the side of the mountain.

From Marsaba our next point was the Dead Sea, called sometimes the Sea of Lot. It is about forty miles long, with an average breadth of nine miles, 1312 feet below the level of the Mediterranean Sea. It is fed by the Jordan and many other streams, but it has no apparent outlet. Its superfluous water is supposed to be carried off entirely by evaporation. The water is characterized by vast quantities of magnesia and soda salts.

The River of Jordan is the principal river of Palestine; it would be considered by an American as an insignificant river. It has a course of 150 miles and enters into the Dead Sea. It is the most historical river in the world; indeed, it is the history that clusters round the River Jordan which gives it its prominence.

Jericho is about an hour's ride from Jordan River. It was in this road from Jerusalem to Jericho that the traveller fell among thieves, who stripped, wounded him and left him for dead. Jericho was long celebrated for its beautiful groves and gardens, which were given to Cleopatra by Marc Antony. It is now a barren waste, no beauty nor comeliness about it. From Jerusalem to Jericho is a ride of about nine hours.

From thence we wended our way to Bethany, the home of Lazarus, Mary and Martha. It is a little city not far from Jerusalem. Our next trip was made to Nazareth, by way of Gibeah of Saul, Ramah of Benjamin, and Bethel, where Jacob saw the ladder, while sleeping with his head resting upon a stone. Jacob's well is here, where Christ held the conversation with the woman; Nebulus, or an ancient city of Shechem, between Mount Ebal and Mount Gerizim; the Plain of Esdraelon, and the Lake of Galilee.

In Nazareth, like most of the other towns of Palestine, the houses are built of stone, with flat roofs on the ancient order. Here lived Joseph and Mary with their son Jesus. Here Jesus spent his boyhood, roaming over the hills and doubtless carrying water from the famous well. The workshop of Joseph is here, where we are told Jesus, himself, labored.

Coming back to America was probably disappointing. He was back amidst racial unrest. But he continued with his conferences to make America a place for all people to live in unity.

He fought with a great company of people who wanted the same things. It didn't matter to him whether they were Negro or White. Later in his book, he lists some of the White people who helped him - Abraham Lincoln topped the list.

I was excited when I learned he wanted to work on was the Plessy vs Ferguson case. His life was cut short at age 58, but that case continued. The law required that the schools be separate but equal. This resulted in most schools in the 17 segregated states being separate but *not* equal.

That case later became the Brown vs Board of Education lawsuit, in which members of his family were involved. I and two of my siblings became plaintiffs. So, all of his concerns about school segregation were addressed and changed through legislation in 1954. Being a Christian, I know it was God who brought it to pass.

There is another side of my mother's family. Her father was a famous basketball player in the Negro League. His name was Hudson Jones Oliver. Ancestry.com provides this snapshot of Hudson Oliver's life captured by the 1940 U.S. Census. Hudson Oliver was born in about 1890. In 1940, he was 50 years old and lived in New York City with his wife, Owille, son, and daughter.

Hudson "Huddy" Oliver was a four-time winner of the Colored Basketball World Championship with three different teams — the Smart Set Athletic Club, the Washington 12 Streeters, and Howard University. Oliver was universally considered the best Colored basketball player.

> "Mr. Hudson Oliver has amazed the public by his wonderful playing and is looked upon as the best player of the six colored teams."
>
> — *The New York Age, 1909*

Hudson 'Huddy' Oliver

He played for the following teams: Jersey City Athletic Club, Smart Set Athletic Club, Washington 12 Streeters, and Howard University. Hudson "Huddy" Oliver was a four-time winner of the Colored Basketball World Championship with three different teams — the Smart Set Athletic Club, the Washington 12 Streeters, and Howard University.

Oliver was universally considered the best Colored basketball player prior to the early 1910s. This, along with his championship titles, makes him one of the most deserving candidates from the early years of the Black Fives Era for inclusion in the Basketball Hall of Fame.

After graduating from Howard University, where he also attended medical school while playing varsity basketball, Oliver became a doctor. Dr. Hudson J. Oliver interned at Freedman's Hospital before beginning his career as a physician in Asbury Park, New Jersey. He moved to Harlem in 1921, where he became a prominent physician and would practice medicine for 34 years, including a stint on the staff at Harlem Hospital.

Dr. Oliver remained active in basketball, mostly coaching some women's teams in the mid-1920s. He was a military veteran and an officer in the Knights of Columbus and was also the exalted ruler of the Monarch Elks Lodge in Harlem. He died in Harlem in 1955.

The stories of these two great men exemplify the standards and accomplishments of some of my family members and many others in the Black community during that period.

CHAPTER 11
MIRCULOUS
PROTECTION ON
9/11

I was still working at the AICPA, which had relocated to New Jersey before 9/11 happened. I usually traveled to work either on the ferry or on the train called The Path, which passed through the lower level of the World Trade Center at approximately 8:45a.m. each day. I could never get up in time to leave any earlier. In May, before 9/11, I started to wake up early. I felt it was the Lord. The first day, I was wide awake and got up to get ready for work. I took my time for prayer and Bible reading. I then started my commute to work. I had a choice of transportation.

The Ferry was the best way because it was an enjoyable trip across the Hudson River. However, to reach the river, I had to enter the North World Trade Center Tower, Building 1, and take an elevator to the basement, then exit to the Pier area where I caught the ferry. Other days, I would go into

Building 5 then down several levels to The Path. It was a long trip down and a long trip on The Path through the tunnel to get to my job in New Jersey.

The reason I was waking up early was always a mystery to me. I didn't know why, but I was able to leave for work early every day thereafter. My company was going into their fiscal year-end close in July, so I thought that must be the reason.

After the close ended in August, I expected to go back to my old wake-up time, but I couldn't. I still woke up early and went to work. It wasn't until 9/11 that I understood why. I should have died that day, but because God had changed my commute pattern, I had divine protection.

It was a horrific event, very difficult to describe. Fortunately, our entire staff was safe. We had to remain in New Jersey for the night. Our company secured hotel rooms for us. That night many of us gathered for prayer.

There was tremendous support as we stayed close to each other and to Jesus. We remained in a state of shock, though, and walked around Jersey City. We found a place to buy food and other needs.

Many of the staff actually saw the towers come down. I was spared seeing them collapse. Later, we all stood on the dock and watched the towers in ruins. There were ferries docking and the people arriving wore such somber expressions.

The next day, I was able to get back into the city. There were two locations for The Path train. The one in lower Manhattan was flooded from the water flowing from the destruction. But there was another one that was still running into mid-town.

We were able to commute each day to work in New Jersey. When we got back to our jobs, we continued to pray every day. We gathered in the aisles and lifted our prayers to Jesus. Many people in other companies in our building also did the same. Bible studies started in the lobbies. No one stopped these spiritual gatherings.

It was a rare time of unity in America.

When I got back to New York for the first time, a shock awaited me. Everywhere I looked, there were signs: "God Bless America" and "In God We Trust." The city was plastered with these signs along with thousands of American flags. The homeless men on the streets were singing and playing their instruments to "God Bless America." I couldn't believe this was New York City. I hoped this was how it would always be. One of the most incredible things was a perfect cross made of steel beams that workers had found in the rubble and put on a high place for all to see.

Every day during those times, I gave thanks to the Lord for protecting us. He is good.

Everyday life, now, at my job was interesting. It was so very different. My commute included going through airport type security, through metal detectors. It was also like a constant remembrance of what had happened. Signs and billboards were everywhere. The ferries were renamed to the people who had lost their lives. Some days I would cry.

The best route for me was by ferry, but it was a challenge. A platform had been constructed at the Pier at the end of lower Manhattan. The only problem with it was it was constantly moving. I called it the moving platform. Also, there was a ladder to get to it. Both were moving in different directions. I had to walk down the ladder and time my jump to reach the moving platform. Once there, I did a dance to the docks, supporting myself by grabbing hold of air. Once at my gate, I was able to grab some rope and wait for the ferry to slam into the moving platform. The waters were always rough at the end of Manhattan. The captain had to dock in two stages. I did another dance to walk the plank and get inside the ferry. Once seated, it was a fairly nice trip. That was until we got to the Jersey City pier where on rare times there was a semblance of sneaky waves. These were rogue waves that came suddenly and sprayed those on the pier. But I got used to the commute and so did others. We traded stories of our unusual trips. Once a lady told me the ferry was coming into the dock too fast, and all went home soaking wet. Whatever circumstances came to me, I learned to trust Jesus.

"The angel of the Lord encampeth round about them that fear him, and delivereth them." Psalm 34:7 NKJ

CHAPTER 12 GOD'S FAVOR PACKAGE

Everything looks bright with God in the midst. While there have been many difficult experiences, today's outlook is very good and full of divine favor. The year 2022 started out with unexpected events and was exciting, shocking, and full of miracles. The title of this book is apropos as I did have a miraculous recovery from the neglect I suffered during my first year of life. From experiencing desegregation, the Brown v Board of Education activities, my experiences in attending college in Boston, becoming a television actress in New York, my life has been very eventful – even with my crazy chicken story and my battle with the cookie monster.

The year 2021 ended with my retirement as a full-time employee from my job at Landor. It was bittersweet, because I had worked there for 14 years and loved it. However, since January 2022, I worked there in a part-time capacity, which was perfect as almost immediately, I began to travel for speaking engagements and events concerning the Brown vs Board of Education case. It was so sudden, it almost took my breath away.

Five states were in the Brown v. Board of Education case which included Kansas, Delaware, Washington, D.C., Virginia and South Carolina. Kansas was shown to be the first state to appeal to the Supreme Court, and so it was the first state to create a museum within the National Park Service in Topeka honoring the integration of schools. The other four states sought the same status as Kansas.

The first event was a webinar which was something completely new to me. It was to aid the effort and took place on March 30, 2022, with people from Delaware telling their stories of desegregationm . There were several dress rehearsals, going over what I would say, checking lighting and other technical things, and meeting new people, especially former students from Howard High and Hockessin Elementary schools. It went well, and I gained experience. It seemed to me that I was moving in a different direction than what I had been doing previously. And that was good.

We also had another webinar with the National Trust for Historic Preservation in Topeka, Kansas including people from all five states. It was an interesting event where I and others shared more stories.

The plan was that Delaware and the other three states that were part of the Brown case would also be able to have an exhibit in a museum with assistance from the National Park Service. The bill was generated and called the Brown v Board of Education National Historical Park Expansion and Redesignation Act (S,270). This would provide venues to enable students from the other states to display and tell their stories.

"Behold I will do a new thing. Now it shall spring forth." Isaiah 43:19 KJV

For years, our historians had tried to bring our case in alignment with the Kansas case. The other 4 cases had the same issue. Everything centered around the Kansas case. The rest of us were called the et al. Our stories had gone unheard. But now, 70 years later for Claymont and 68 years for the other three, things were changing. Delaware Senators became involved, generating that bill, which was then sent to both the House and Senate for a vote. The bill stated that the four states could create a museum with exhibits within the Park Services. Those of us from Delaware were so happy. My story and others were continually ignored had been upsetting. This was a happy occasion though. The bill passed the Senate and the House.

The bill was sent to the president for signature, and I was invited to the ceremony. Those from Delaware and other states attended. May 12, 2022, was an exciting day. I had never in my life met a president. I was able to shake hands with both him and the vice president. After he signed the bill, his people came to take him to his next event, but he lingered. He wanted to stay and chat with us. Being from Delaware, he knew the case. So, he waved us over to the other side of the oval office, where there were sofas and chairs. His people kept nudging him, but he kept waving them off. Finally, he said goodbye.

We were then given a royal tour of the White House and the building that housed the library and rooms named different colors. I even got to ride in the president's private elevator. It was either that or walk up a long winding staircase. We didn't get to see the living quarters, but we were in the kitchen and saw food preparation. We were given a large cookie with the presidential seal on it. It was delicious. But I was already healed of the monster cookie, so I didn't get addicted.

Overall, it was an outstanding adventure. Mostly because the bill was signed, and we were now part of the park services along with Kansas. Now people from all over could hear our stories as well. The long wait was worth it.

Joan addressing students at Claymont High School, September, 2022.

The next event was Claymont's 70 anniversary celebration, which took place on September 15-16, 2022. I was one of the speakers. On Thursday, I spoke to 800 elementary school children at Claymont elementary school. At first, I thought they meant I would speak before 80 students. When I realized that there really would be was 800, I was scared, and couldn't sleep that night. I prayed and found comfort in the word which says "For I the Lord thy God will hold thy right hand saying unto me fear not I will help you." Isaiah 41:13 KJV. That gave me great comfort. When Thursday arrived, I was ushered in to an 800-seat auditorium - a little frightening, but I remained calm. Friends and family had prayed for me. The school had grades kindergarten through 6th grade. The 4th and 5th graders were brought into the auditorium. Due to COVID instructions, they were spread apart, and the other students watched a live feed into their classrooms.

It turned out to be a fun event. They were very good and well mannered. They laughed a lot and clapped a lot. I used the opportunity to tell my famous pet chicken story. I first asked them how many had pets. They all raised their hands. I then asked how many had a pet chicken. Several raised their hands. So, I proceeded to tell them the story of my pet chicken and how he ended up on my plate one evening. Our parents had served us our pet for dinner.

I also shared with them what the times were like in my era. In many places, the races were divided, and that neither race wanted integration, except for Claymont High. I explained their history and how Claymont fought for integration and did some things that were illegal to achieve it.

They needed to understand their history, how the Claymont high School Board met with the Black parents and asked them if they wanted their children to attend the school. They said yes, which was the beginning of the Delaware lawsuit.

I shared that there was a strong bond between the family and church. And if it weren't for that, we would have seen ourselves as 2nd class citizens. In those days church was of prime importance. Everything took place there, weekly services, Sunday school, socials, dances, rummage sales. I continued to tell them what it was like entering Claymont - an all-White school, and how well we were received and fit in. They laughed when I said I joined the glee club, but I couldn't sing on key. They also laughed when I said I was the pitcher for the softball team and pitched the first ball over the fence, and also couldn't get the ball in the basket when on the basketball team.

I gave them an example of how well the races got along. Our football team played another team out of state. After the game, they went to a place to eat. There were Black players on the team, and the waitress refused to serve them. So, the whole team got up and left. That was the kind of unity we had at Claymont. I ended my talk with "Love God, love your neighbor and do acts of kindness." The children thoroughly enjoyed themselves, and so did I. They were well mannered for which I was thankful. I was showered with standing ovations and gifts. After a week, the flowers were still blooming. I remember the scripture which says, "So shalt thou find favour and good understanding in the sight of God and man." Proverbs 3:4 KJV. Thats how I would describe that day. I was given so much favor, more that I would have imagine. Praise the Lord!

As I reflect on this day, it is one I will always remember. It ended with a nice dinner with my friend Allison David who is the CEO of the Claymont Community center (the old high school) and her family.

It was my beautiful day on Thursday. And Friday was coming next-another exciting day. It was the actual day of the 70th celebration.

Since Claymont High was closed many years ago, the building is now the Claymont Community Center. It houses day care, senior citizen activities, and the Claymont High school exhibits. The displays were exciting to view. There were pictures of the Claymont 12, which included me. Friday morning Allison and I went to the Community Center as the finishing touches were being done. Guests for the celebration started arriving around 8:30 am. There were senators, and other elected officials and many who were familiar with the lawsuit. It was then that I was told I was the featured speaker. I was a little shocked. "The Lord bestows favor and honor." Psalm 84:11 KJV. The other speaker was Senator Coons, who I met at the White House, and was happy to sit next to and chat with.

Jesus had told me before I arrived in Claymont not to figure out what I was to say. He gave me some bullet points of things to go over, but not to decide verbatim what to say. He wanted me to rely completely on Him and let his words flow through me. I believe that's what happened. I spoke his words that were right for the events.

Later as reporters were interviewing me, I was asked a question that I had thought about myself. How is it that so many people in Claymont fought for integration when in other places they didn't. I answered that I was a Christian and had prayed about that, and there are seasons where people are born for such a time. I continued to say, I was born for this time. I was amazed that all of my spiritual words were not deleted by the Press but were included in the online video. I could feel the Christians there, favoring me.

I had not had that many interviews and requests for pictures before. Things were a first for me, but I could feel Jesus with me, keeping me calm. I was happy that I didn't withdraw in any way, but was proactive in speaking to people, especially the children. I can see that things were continuing to improve in my healing process. My pastor has often said "We are all called to do great things, but we cannot do them alone." I have come to rely on wisdom and prayers from family and friends.

One nice thing was that many of the children from the Thursday event also came to the Friday one. I had time to chat with them and answer their questions. I wish I could have taken some of them home with me. They were beautiful.

I really saw the favor of Jesus in my life in this trip. Everything worked to perfection.

It's time to move on to my next trip, which took place on September 28 through October 1, 2022, at Topeka Kansas. This was a next step to get the four states set up in the park service.

People from these states came to learn how and what to do. There were webinars, museum trips and social event. We had a bus at our disposal which took us to the various places. Some of the speakers talked to us onboard these bus trips. There were many companies and speakers who provided us the information we needed. It was a tight schedule, but all worked out. We felt empowered to proceed. We also developed a bond to work together and stay in touch. We ate together and talked much. We were given a list of our contact information, so we could stay in touch, which we are doing.

I was happy to meet many Christians there and sense Jesus' presence. I could feel the prayers that went up for us. Even though it was a little tiring, it was exciting. We will be meeting again in each of our sites and by webinars. I look forward to them, and I know the others felt the same way.

There was just one unusual thing that happened in the hotel where we stayed. There was a dog show in town. And our hotel housed 400 of them.

I can't begin to tell you what that was like. There was a lot of barking, howling, and having to share the elevators with them. But I didn't really get upset about it. I was still able to sleep at nights, probably because of our long daily schedules. In fact, the dog next door howled a lot and I felt bad for it. I could feel it was frightened. Having had a pet dog myself, I could sympathize. But we were all happy to leave. We still had the smell of them in us for quite some time.

This dog tale reminds me of another that I had on a previous flight home from Memphis, TN. It was my brother Victor's 50th wedding anniversary celebration. It was a very special event with many family members in attendance. I got on my plane and sat next to the window in a 3-seat row. A couple arrived with a dog. It was large. So, there we were, with 3 adults and one dog trying to fit in a small seat row, which was impossible to do. They assured me that the dog would sleep through the whole journey. That didn't happen. It started moving around. But there was no place for it to move around. It ended up against my leg. And I couldn't move.

Finally the plane landed, but I was horrified to think how I could get out. There was no room, and my luggage was in the overhead bin. The couple first thought about backing the dog out into the aisle. But if they did that, they would have to back it up the aisle and back it out of the plane door. A crowd was forming behind the man. Everyone wanted to get out. He brought my luggage down and then worked on getting the dog turned around, which was impossible to do. It looked .like we were all stuck including my suitcase. Finally, the man was able to move and switch the four of us around and got us out. I breathed a sigh of relief when I left the plane, praying this would never happen again.

So, my trip home from Kansas was eventful. There was an act of kindness on the plane. The person in charge of when the planes take off, delayed our leaving, to wait for two other planes to land and for the passengers and luggage to reach ours. If the person in charge had not done that, those people would not have been able to leave until the next day. It was worth the delay. Also, I was again favored with a quick trip home from LGA, because it was a fast flight and arrived close to on time.

This is the end of my journey to a miraculous recovery in Jesus. I've fully recovered. My life is still moving on and into my future. I continue to grow and to check myself, so I don't go back into old habits of unforgiveness and retreating into myself, away from people. In my Church, Faith Exchange, we are a close-knit family. We have to give voice and speak up about ourselves. It causes me stay out there and not lay back but be proactive in ministering to other people. As part of the intercessory prayer group, we all take turns praying for others. I pray and read my Bible daily, especially the red letters of Jesus speaking in the Gospels. I write them, because it's like He is standing in front of me saying those words. I do everything I can do to stay close to Him, because He loves me and stays close to me. He saved me and now "He is in me, and I am in Him." John 17:23 KJV. My future is bright.

I feel good about myself today. I am a happy, joyful person, and have fun being around others. I've had so many wonderful events in my life. They point me to a loving God, full of favor, mercy and grace. I'm so very excited to experience what is ahead. I know Thanksgiving and Christmas are coming and I will spend time with family and friends. I will also work on and plan for my 2024 vision and goals. I know Brown vs Board events will happen along with possible speaking engagements. I also know that in the future there will be more of His Favor towards me. "A man's gift makes room for him and brings him before great men." Prov 18:16 KJV

"Are you weary, carrying a heavy burden? Come to me. I will refresh your life, for I am your oasis. Simply join your life with mine. Learn my ways and you'll discover that I'm gentle, humble, easy to please. You will find refreshment and rest in me. For all that I require of you will be pleasant and easy to bear." Matthew 11:28-30 KJV Passion Translation

ABOUT THE
AUTHOR

 Joan Elizabeth Anderson was born in 1938 to Dr. Leon and Beulah Anderson in Wilmington, Delaware, where she and her siblings lived for many years. She attended Wilmington Elementary and Howard High Schools. The Anderson family moved to Ardencroft, a suburb of Claymont, Delaware in 1952. She attended Claymont High School and became part of the Brown v Board of Education lawsuit. After graduation, she attended Fisk University for two years and then transferred to and graduated from Boston University in 1960. New York was her next and last stop. She worked as an actress on soap operas, a counselor in a drug rehabilitation center, accounting departments at AICPA, major league baseball and Landor. In 1978, she graduated from

the L.I. Bible School, and taught Sunday School classes. Presently, Joan is a writer and motivational speaker.

ACKNOWLEDGMENTS

I truly am thankful for my parents, who did whatever they could to help me. They both came to New York, sometimes separately, to visit me. I had a good relationship with them in my adulthood. I love them so much.

I am also thankful for my friends Joyce, Carol, Norma, and Judy- my steady lifelong friends, who gave me great support and helped me overcome my past.

Denice Cassino is my Book Coach and Publicist, who spent much time teaching and helping me with the difficult task of writing my autobiography. She is fabulous.

There were several people who helped me with my writings. I am so very happy with their support:

Jan Ford - Editor

Juanita Edwards– designer

Collette

Kendra Siebert – photographer

Julie Doughty –Editor and Picture captions-L&F

Phil Hodges - old photo enhancements-L&F

Without their expertise, this would not be a quality book.

Last, but not lease, I am thankful to my pastors-Dan and Annie Stratton, who gave me tremendous spiritual and emotional support. Many church members also helped me. I am blessed.

FOREWORD

It is hard to imagine the world Joan E. Anderson grew up in. School integration was illegal nationwide until courageous leaders made some strong decisions to change education here in the United States. Joan's family moved to Ardencroft, Delaware to be part of this nation-changing movement. With candor she shares her experience attending Black schools, primarily White schools where she was one of the very few laBck students and later integrated schools. She does so without an agenda. She simply describes her experience, and with surprising gratitude, she expresses her appreciation for those brave enough to step forward and fight for quality education for all students, regardless of ethnicity.

Joan's voice is a necessary voice in the era of DEI - Diversity, Equity and Inclusion. Her story talks about the favor she received throughout her life. Doors were open to her and she walked through them. She was encouraged by her family to pursue higher education, which she did. She describes herself as a slow learner, but with her life experience - seeing things that seemed impossible happen, she traveled to Boston and then to New York

City to put her skills, her talents and her willingness to work on the line to see if she could succeed. And she did succeed.

Joan credits the hand of God for her success. In retrospect, she sees where His hand guided her through every trial and circumstance. Today, she serves God as an intercessor and as an example to people of all ages and ethnicities. I am proud to be her pastor at this time in her life.

She carries with her the same optimism and energy she did throughout her life. She is now an author and a public speaker, speaking throughout the country about her experiences during the integration process leading up to the now famous Brown vs. the Board of Education case. She speaks of some of the early civil rights leaders as family friends. If you ever get a chance to meet her, you will be glad you did. She is filled with hope and renewed excitement and she is an encouragement to everyone she meets and especially to young people of color.

Daniel J. Stratton, Senior Pastor

Faith Exchange Fellowship

New York City

www.ingramcontent.com/pod-product-compliance
Lightning Source LLC
Chambersburg PA
CBHW071205120626
46546CB00006B/2427